PROBLEM SOLVING
Step by Step

Copyright © 1999 Metropolitan Teaching and Learning Company. All rights reserved. No part of this book may be reproduced or utilized in any form or by any means, electronic or mechanical, including photocopying, recording, or by any information storage and retrieval system without permission in writing from the publisher. For information regarding permission, write to the address below.

Metropolitan Teaching and Learning Company
33 Irving Place
New York, New York 10003

Cover photographs: Robin Prange/The Stock Market
Printed in the United States of America

ISBN: 1-58120-706-9
10 9 8 7 6 5 4 3

STEP 6 • Table of Contents

CHAPTER 1 • WHOLE NUMBERS AND DECIMALS
Lesson 1	Find Needed Information—*Using a Table*	5–8
Lesson 2	Decide on the Kind of Answer You Need—*Answering the Question*	9–12
Lesson 3	Decide What to Do First—*Eliminating Unreasonable Possibilities*	13–16

CHAPTER 2 • OPERATIONS WITH WHOLE NUMBERS
Lesson 1	Show Information Another Way—*Writing a Word Equation*	17–20
Lesson 2	Decide What to Do First—*Solving Multi-Step Problems*	21–24
Lesson 3	Show Information Another Way—*Making a Table to Generalize*	25–28
Lesson 4	Decide on the Kind of Answer You Need—*Deciding Whether to Estimate*	29–32
	Test-Taking Skill: *Writing a Plan*	33–34

CHAPTER 3 • OPERATIONS WITH DECIMALS
Lesson 1	Show Information Another Way—*Writing a Word Equation*	35–38
Lesson 2	Decide on the Kind of Answer You Need—*Interpreting Quotients*	39–42
Lesson 3	Show Information Another Way—*Using Simpler Numbers*	43–46
Lesson 4	Show Information Another Way—*Solving a Missing Factor Problem*	47–50

CHAPTER 4 • DEALING WITH DATA
Lesson 1	Find Needed Information—*Underlining Needed information*	51–54
Lesson 2	Find Needed Information—*Interpreting Changes in a Line Graph*	55–58
Lesson 3	Find Needed Information—*Reading a Double-Bar Graph*	59–62
Lesson 4	Find Needed Information—*Reading a Double-Line Graph*	63–66
	Test-Taking Skill: *Eliminating Choices*	67–68

CHAPTER 5 • EXPRESSIONS AND INTEGERS
Lesson 1	Show Information Another Way—*Writing an Equation*	69–72
Lesson 2	Show Information Another Way—*Drawing a Number Line*	73–76
Lesson 3	Show Information Another Way—*Drawing a Picture*	77–80

CHAPTER 6 • FRACTIONS AND MIXED NUMBERS
Lesson 1	Show Information Another Way—*Drawing a Number Line*	81–84
Lesson 2	Find Needed Information—*Underlining Needed Information*	85–88
Lesson 3	Decide What to Do First—*Solving Multi-Step Problems*	89–92
	Test-Taking Skill: *Writing a Plan*	93–94

CHAPTER 7 • RATIO AND PROPORTION

Lesson 1	Show Information Another Way—*Writing a Word Equation*	95–98
Lesson 2	Show Information Another Way—*Writing Word Proportions*	99–102
Lesson 3	Decide on the Kind of Answer You Need—*Using Unit Rates*	103–106
Lesson 4	Show Information Another Way—*Making a Rate Graph*	107–110

CHAPTER 8 • PERCENT

Lesson 1	Find Needed Information—*Using an Order Form*	111–114
Lesson 2	Decide What to Do First—*Percents, Fractions, and Decimals*	115–118
Lesson 3	Show Information Another Way—*Writing Percent Equations*	119–122
Lesson 4	Decide on the Kind of Answer You Need—*Estimating Percents*	123–126
Lesson 5	Decide What to Do First—*Solving Multi-Step Percent Problems*	127–130
	Test-Taking Skill: *Visualizing the Problem*	131–132

CHAPTER 9 • USING FORMULAS

Lesson 1	Decide on the Kind of Answer You Need—*Choosing the Unit*	133–136
Lesson 2	Show Information Another Way—*Choosing the Formula*	137–140
Lesson 3	Find Needed Information—*Solving Multi-Step Problems*	141–144
Lesson 4	Show Information Another Way—*Rewriting a Formula*	145–148

CHAPTER 10 • MEASUREMENT

Lesson 1	Decide What to Do First—*Renaming Measures*	149–152
Lesson 2	Decide on the Kind of Answer You Need—*Interpreting Remainders*	153–156
	Test-Taking Skill: *Writing a Plan*	157–158

CHAPTER 11 • GEOMETRY

Lesson 1	Show Information Another Way—*Drawing a Picture*	159–162
Lesson 2	Find Needed Information—*Solving a Problem Within the Problem*	163–166

CHAPTER 12 • PROBABILITY

Lesson 1	Show Information Another Way—*Making an Organized List*	167–170
Lesson 2	Show Information Another Way—*Making a Tree Diagram*	171–174
	Test-Taking Skill: *Trying Out the Answer Choices*	175–176

STEP 6 • Topics

TABLES
1.1 Using a Table
1.3 Eliminating Unreasonable Possibilities
2.3 Making a Table to Generalize
4.1 Underlining Needed Information
6.2 Underlining Needed Information

BAR GRAPHS
4.3 Reading a Double-Bar Graph

LINE GRAPHS
4.2 Interpreting Changes in a Line Graph
4.4 Reading a Double-Line Graph
7.4 Making a Rate Graph

MULTI-STEP PROBLEMS
2.1 Writing a Word Equation
2.2 Solving Multi-Step Problems
3.1 Writing a Word Equation
6.3 Solving Multi-Step Problems
8.5 Solving Multi-Step Percent Problems
9.3 Solving Multi-Step Problems
11.2 Solving a Problem Within the Problem

ESTIMATION/NUMBER SENSE
1.2 Answering the Question
1.3 Eliminating Unreasonable Possibilities
2.4 Deciding Whether to Estimate
6.1 Drawing a Number Line
8.4 Estimating Percents
9.1 Choosing the Unit
9.2 Choosing the Formula

REPRESENTING PROBLEMS DIFFERENTLY
2.1 Writing a Word Equation
3.1 Writing a Word Equation
3.3 Using Simpler Numbers
3.4 Solving a Missing Factor Problem
5.1 Writing an Equation
7.1 Writing a Word Equation
7.2 Writing Word Proportions
8.2 Percents, Fractions, and Decimals
8.3 Writing Percent Equations
9.4 Rewriting a Formula
10.1 Renaming Measures

PROPORTIONAL THINKING
7.1 Writing a Word Equation
7.2 Writing Word Proportions
7.3 Using Unit Rates
7.4 Making a Rate Graph

ALGEBRAIC THINKING
2.1 Writing a Word Equation
2.3 Deciding Whether to Estimate
3.1 Writing a Word Equation
3.4 Solving a Missing Factor Problem
5.1 Writing an Equation
7.1 Writing a Word Equation
7.2 Writing Word Proportions
8.3 Writing Percent Equations
9.2 Choosing the Formula
9.3 Solving Multi-Step Problems
9.4 Rewriting a Formula
11.2 Solving a Problem Within the Problem

VISUAL THINKING
4.1 Underlining Needed Information
5.2 Drawing a Number Line
5.3 Drawing a Picture
6.1 Drawing a Number Line
6.2 Underlining Needed Information
7.4 Making a Rate Graph
11.1 Drawing a Picture
12.1 Making an Organized List
12.2 Making a Tree Diagram

ANSWER INTERPRETATION
1.2 Answering the Question
1.3 Eliminating Unreasonable Possibilities
2.4 Deciding Whether to Estimate
3.2 Interpreting Quotients
10.2 Interpreting Remainders

RECOGNIZING IMPORTANT INFORMATION
1.1 Using a Table
4.1 Underlining Needed Information
6.2 Underlining Needed Information
8.1 Using an Order Form

Chapter 1 | **L1**

Using a Table

Sometimes the information you need to solve a problem is presented in a table.

Trailrail: Schedule as of 9/01/99				
Colton	06:45*	07:45*	08:45	11:10
Amville	06:55*	07:55*	08:55	
Taunton	07:10*	08:10*	09:10	
Ibbing	07:42*	08:42*	09:42	11:55
Newchester	08:05*	09:05*	10:05	12:18

* Monday through Friday only

> In a train schedule, each column of the table shows the times that one train makes stops. This schedule shows the stops made by morning trains from Colton to Newchester.

Example 1

How long does the train take to travel from Taunton to Newchester?

Step 1: Find Taunton on the table.
At what times does the train leave Taunton? _____

Step 2: Find Newchester on the schedule.
At what times does the train reach Newchester? _____

Step 3: Find the time difference between the two stations.
Is the time between the two stations the same for each train? _____

It takes the train _____ to go from Taunton to Newchester.

Example 2

What is the earliest train leaving Amville for Newchester on Saturday?

Step 1: Look at the schedule to find out about Saturday trains.

What does an asterisk (*) on the schedule mean?

_____

Step 2: Find the columns that show Saturday trains.

The earliest train on Saturday leaves Amville at _____.

Example 3

What is the least time the train takes to travel from Colton to Ibbing?

Step 1: Compare the times taken between the two stations.

Which train takes the least time? _____

Step 2: Find the time difference between the stations.

The least time from Colton to Ibbing is _____.

• Elapsed Time

5

GUIDED PRACTICE

The table shows the price per gross of various bolts in three different metals. The first measurement of each bolt is its diameter, and the second is its length. Use the table to solve the problems.

Machined Bolts—Hexagonal Head: Price per gross						
	$\frac{1}{4}" \times \frac{3}{4}"$	$\frac{1}{4}" \times 1"$	$\frac{1}{4}" \times 1\frac{1}{2}"$	$\frac{3}{8}" \times \frac{3}{4}"$	$\frac{3}{8}" \times 1"$	$\frac{3}{8}" \times 1\frac{1}{2}"$
Standard	$7.12	$8.09	$9.25	$8.40	$9.45	$11.32
Steel	$16.40	$18.60	$21.28	$19.32	$21.75	$26.00
Brass	$12.90	$14.56	$16.65	$15.12	$17.00	$20.38

1. How much more per gross do $\frac{1}{4}" \times 1\frac{1}{2}"$ brass bolts cost than the same size standard bolts?

   a. Find the column for $\frac{1}{4}" \times 1\frac{1}{2}"$ bolts.

   Run your finger across the row for standard bolts.

   How much does a gross of standard $\frac{1}{4}" \times 1\frac{1}{2}"$ bolts cost? _____

   b. Run your finger across the row for brass bolts.

   How much does a gross of brass $\frac{1}{4}" \times 1\frac{1}{2}"$ bolts cost? _____

   c. Calculate the difference in price.

   _____ − _____ = _____

   So, the brass bolts cost _____ more than the standard bolts.

2. How much would it cost to buy a gross of steel $\frac{1}{4}" \times 1"$ bolts and a gross of steel $\frac{3}{8}" \times 1"$ bolts?

   a. Find the row for steel bolts.

   Run your finger along the row until you reach the $\frac{1}{4}" \times 1"$ column.

   How much does a gross of bolts cost? _____

   b. **How much does a gross of $\frac{3}{8}" \times 1"$ bolts cost?** _____

   c. Calculate the total cost.

   _____ + _____ = _____

   So, the bolts would cost _____ .

Chapter 1 L1

PRACTICE

The table shows the sales of three video games at a store over a one-year period. Use the table to solve the problems.

Video Game Sales at Sonny's Techstore, 1999				
	Jan. through Mar.	Apr through Jun.	Jul. through Sep.	Oct. through Dec.
Submarine	$10,488	$8,604	$7,590	$12,044
Planet 9	$2340	$1,865	$1,678	$2,584
The Defender	$0	$5,063	$7,279	$13,006

3. Which of the video games had the greatest sales for the year? How can you tell?

   _____
   _____
   _____

4. How much did the store earn from the video games sales January through March? How did you find out?

   _____
   _____
   _____

5. During which period are sales of video games the highest at Sonny's Techstore? Can you explain why?

   _____
   _____
   _____
   _____

6. What can you tell about the sales of Planet 9 during May? Explain your answer.

   _____
   _____
   _____
   _____

7. One of the video games first came on the market in May, 1999. Which one was it? How can you tell?

   _____
   _____
   _____
   _____

8. Was the video game introduced in May popular or unpopular? How can you tell from the table?

   _____
   _____
   _____
   _____

• Elapsed Time

TEST-TAKING PRACTICE

Daily Flights From Jennings To Madrid City				
	Flight 731	Flight 704	Flight 1262	Flight 790
Leave Jennings	8:10 AM	11:10 AM	2:40 PM	5:20 PM
Arrive San Miguel	10:15 AM	1:15 PM		7:25 PM
	Flight 912	Flight 982		Flight 940
Leave San Miguel	10:45 AM	1:45 PM		7:55 PM
Arrive Madrid City	1:05 PM	4:05 PM	6:00 PM	10:15 PM

Some of the flights from Jennings to Madrid City, on the schedule above, involve a change of planes in San Miguel. Use the schedule to answer the questions. Fill in the answer box of your choice in the section at the bottom of the page.

1. If you wanted to fly from Jennings directly to Madrid City, without stopping on the way, which flight would you take?
   A Flight 704
   B Flight 731
   C Flight 790
   D Flight 1262

2. How long does the flight from Jennings to San Miguel take?
   J 1 hour 5 minutes
   K 2 hours 5 minutes
   L 2 hours 35 minutes
   M 4 hours 55 minutes

3. How much less time does it take to travel from Jennings to Madrid City if you don't stop over at San Miguel?
   A 35 minutes less
   B 1 hour 5 minutes less
   C 1 hours 35 minutes less
   D Not Given

4. Jane took Flight 704, but missed her connection in San Miguel. She took the next flight from San Miguel. When did she reach Madrid City?

   J 1:05 PM   L 6:00 PM
   K 4:05 PM   M 10:15 PM

Write About It

5. If you had to be in Madrid City at 11:15 on Tuesday morning, which flight from Jennings would you take so that you wasted as little time as possible? Explain.

   _____
   _____
   _____
   _____

1. A☐ B☐ C☐ D☐   3. A☐ B☐ C☐ D☐
2. J☐ K☐ L☐ M☐   4. J☐ K☐ L☐ M☐

• Elapsed Time

Answering the Question

However well you compute an answer, it will be incorrect if it answers the wrong question. Before solving a problem, decide what kind of answer the problem requires.

Example 1

Jay earns $6.75 an hour and works 35 hours each week. Robin earns $5.75 an hour and works 40 hours each week. Does Jay earn more than Robin?

Step 1: Read the problem carefully, and decide what kind of answer you should give.

- Does the problem ask for a number? _____
- Does the problem ask which person earns the most? _____
- Does the problem ask for a Yes or a No? _____

Step 2: Decide how to calculate the right answer.

How much does Jay earn each week? $6.75 x 35 = $236.25

How much does Robin earn each week? $5.75 x 40 = $230.00

Step 3: Compare the amounts. $236.25 _____ $230.00

So, the answer is: Yes, Jay earns more than Robin.

Example 2

A morning train service runs from Levley to Barnett. The 6:45 train reaches Barnett at 8:30, and the 7:05 train reaches Barnett at 8:55. How long does the faster train take to complete the trip?

Step 1: Decide what kind of answer you should give.

- Does the problem ask which train is faster? _____
- Does the problem ask for a Yes or a No? _____
- Does the problem ask for a number or amount? _____

Step 2: Decide how to reach the right answer.

How long does the 6:45 train take? _____

How long does the 7:05 train take? _____

Step 3: Compare the amounts. _____ < _____

So, the answer is: The faster train takes _____.

• Multiplying Whole Numbers and Money

GUIDED PRACTICE

1. Admission to the museum is $4 for each adult and $1.50 for children. There are 3 adults and 2 children in the Brown family, and there are 2 adults and 5 children in the Green family. Which family can visit the museum for $15.00?

   J $15.50   **L** The Browns

   K The Greens   **M** $0.50 too much

   a. Decide what kind of answer you should choose.

   Is the answer a number, a name, or a *Yes* or *No*? _____

   So, the correct choice will be _____ or _____.

   b. Find out how much each family will pay.

   Browns: 3 × $4 plus 2 × $1.50 = _____

   Greens: 2 × $4 plus 5 × $1.50 = _____

   The _____ family can visit the museum for $15.00.

   So, the correct answer is _____.

2. Jake cut as many 1 ft 8 in. shelves as he could from a board measuring 6 ft 4 in. long. How many inches of wood were left over?

   J 1 ft 4 in.   **L** 14 in.

   K 3 shelves   **M** 16 in.

   a. Decide what kind of answer you should choose.

   Is the answer a number of shelves, mixed units, or inches?
   _____

   So, the correct choice will be _____ or _____.

   b. Find out how many pieces Jake used and how much was left over.

   Rename the lengths as inches.

   6 ft 4 in. = 76 in.   1 ft 8 in. = _____ in.

   76 ÷ _____ = 3 R _____

   There will be _____ inches left over.

   So, the correct answer is _____.

10

PRACTICE

Solve each problem, making sure that you answer the question that is asked.

3. Individually, postcards sell for $0.75 each. A pack of 6 postcards costs $3.80. How much less expensive is it to buy 6 postcards in a pack?

4. Each day Liam walked 1 mile more than the previous day. He began the 7-day week walking 3 miles. How many miles did Liam walk during the week?

5. Sandy has $35.00 that she has decided to spend on CDs. At the store, CDs are on sale for $8.25 each. Can Sandy buy 4 of the CDs?

6. A science teacher has 1 kg (1,000 g) of calcium carbonate. How many students can do an experiment if each student uses 8 g of the chemical?

7. Sally has twice as much money as Roger, who has twice as much money as Lin, who has $5. How much do they have in all?

8. An airplane travels at 600 miles per hour for 3 hours. How much farther did it travel during the last 2 hours than during the first hour?

9. Haruko arrived at a party at 6:15 and stayed until 8:25. Jan arrived at 6:55 and stayed until 9:00. Who was at the party for the longer time?

10. For every 12 magazines Steve sells, he earns $5 for his school. If he sells 50 magazines, will Steve earn more than $25?

• Multiplying Whole Numbers and Money

TEST-TAKING PRACTICE

Choose the correct answer to each problem. Fill in the answer box of your choice in the section at the bottom of the page.

1. Anthony and Dolores went to the amusement park and spent a total of $25.05. Anthony's share of the cost was $12.55. Which of the two spent more money at the park?
   - A $12.50
   - B $37.60
   - C Anthony
   - D Dolores

2. Each shelf at the library can hold 84 books. The library has 44 shelves that are full and another shelf with 36 books on it. How many more books will it take to fill the 45th shelf?
   - J 8 books
   - K 9 books
   - L 48 books
   - M 3,732 books

3. The adult population of Mayberry is 15,820. In the last town election, 7,965 people voted. Did more than half of
   the population vote in the last election?
   - A Less than half
   - B 7,855 people
   - C Yes
   - D No

4. Sean bought 3 T-shirts for $5.20 each and a hat for $4.50. He paid with one bill—the smallest that would cover his purchases. What did Sean give the cashier before getting change?
   - J $0.10
   - K $20.00
   - L $20.10
   - M Not Given

5. A chemist has a 5-kg (5,000-g) bag of charcoal that she uses to perform 4 experiments. Each experiment requires 800 g of charcoal. How many grams of charcoal does she have left?
   - A Yes
   - B 1,800 g
   - C 3.2 kg
   - D 3,200 g

Write About It

6. John is 5 ft 4 in. tall, and his friend Dave is 3 inches taller. Dave's brother Sam is 6 inches shorter than Dave.

   Complete the problem above with a question about the information given. Then explain what form the answer should be in, and solve the problem, showing your work.

   _____
   _____
   _____
   _____
   _____
   _____

---

1. A ☐ B ☐ C ☐ D ☐
2. J ☐ K ☐ L ☐ M ☐
3. A ☐ B ☐ C ☐ D ☐
4. J ☐ K ☐ L ☐ M ☐
5. A ☐ B ☐ C ☐ D ☐

• Multiplying Whole Numbers and Money

Eliminating Unreasonable Possibilities

You can often eliminate some of the answers to a multiple-choice problem by carefully reading the problem and deciding what to do first.

Melting Points and Boiling Points

Substance	Melting Point	Boiling Point
oxygen	−218.9°C	−182.9°C
ammonia	−77.7°C	−33.4°C
mercury	−38.8°C	356.5°C
iron	1,535°C	2,750°C

> Melting point is the temperature at which a substance changes from solid to liquid. Boiling point is the temperature at which a substance changes from liquid to gas.

Example 1

What is the difference in temperature between the melting point and boiling point of iron?

A −1,215 °C   C 1,215 °C
B 1,210.5 °C   D 4,285 °C

Step 1: Look at each answer choice.

• Choice **A** is a negative number, so it cannot be correct. **Cross out choice A.**

• The difference between the boiling point and the melting point has to be less than 2,750. So, choice **D** cannot be correct. **Cross out choice D.**

Step 2: Now you have only two choices. You can see that the correct answer will be a whole number. So, you can eliminate choice **B**.

Check to make sure that choice C is correct. 2,750 − 1,535 = 1,215

Example 2

Which substances are gases at room temperature?

A mercury and ammonia   C ammonia and iron
B iron and oxygen   D oxygen and ammonia

Step 1: Look at each answer choice.

• Choices **B** and **C** include iron, which you know is not a gas at room temperature. **Cross out choices B and C.**

Step 2: Now check the table for choices **A** and **D**. Which two substances have a boiling point less than room temperature?

_____

So, the correct choice is _____.

• Adding and Subtracting Whole Numbers

GUIDED PRACTICE

Speed of Sound

Medium	Speed in m/s
air	346
water	1,497
wood	3,850
glass	4,540
steel	5,200

Sound travels at different speeds through different mediums. The table shows the speed of sound through various substances, in meters per second.

1. How much faster does sound travel through steel than through wood?

  J 1,350 m/s   **L** 1,450 m/s
  K 1,350 km/h   **M** 5,200 m/s

  a. Look at each answer choice.

    • Choice **K** has the wrong units, so it cannot be correct. **Cross out choice K.**

    • Choice **M** is the speed of sound through steel, so it cannot be the correct answer. **Cross out choice M.**

  b. Find the speeds through steel and wood in the table.

  Subtract to find the correct answer.

  5,200 − _____ = _____

  So, the correct answer is _____.

2. In which medium does sound travel about 3 times as fast as it does in water?

  J air   **L** steel
  K glass   **M** 4,540 m/s

  a. Look at each answer choice.

    • Choice **M** is not a medium, so it cannot be correct. **Cross out choice M.**

    • Choice **J** is a medium through which sound travels slower than through water. **Cross out choice J.**

  b. Find the speed through water in the table.

  Estimate the product.

  3 × _____ is about _____

  Find the medium with the speed closest to your estimate.

  So, the correct answer is _____.

PRACTICE

Use the table to solve problems 3 through 8. You may want to cross out unreasonable answer choices to help you solve the problems.

Instrument	Frequency Range (in Hertz)
Piano	30–4,186
Tuba	55–311
Guitar	80–698
Violin	200–2,093
Piccolo	600–3,729

The table shows the frequency range—from lowest note to highest note—of various instruments.

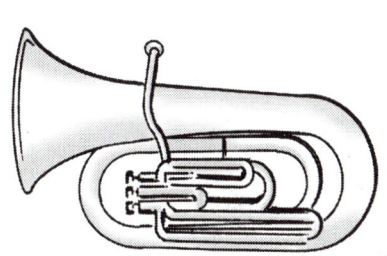

3. Which instrument has the greatest frequency range?

 A 55–311
 B 30–4,186
 C piccolo
 D piano

4. What frequency is the lowest note that can be played on a guitar?

 J 80 Hertz
 K 200 Hertz
 L 311 Hertz
 M tuba

5. Which instrument can reach the highest note?

 A accordion
 B 3729 Hertz
 C piccolo
 D piano

6. Which instrument can reach the lowest note?

 J 30 Hertz
 K tuba
 L string bass
 M piano

7. What is the frequency range of the violin?

 A 80–698 Hertz
 B 2,093 Hertz
 C 200–2,093 Hertz
 D 200–2,100 Hertz

8. Which instrument's highest note is lower than a piccolo's lowest note?

 J piano
 K tuba
 L bass drum
 M 600 Hertz

• Adding and Subtracting Whole Numbers

TEST-TAKING PRACTICE

Choose the correct answer to each problem. Fill in the answer box of your choice in the section at the bottom of the page.

Cenozoic Era   Tertiary Period

Epoch	Millions of Years Ago	
Pliocene	Began 5	Ended 2
Miocene	Began 23	Ended 5
Oligocene	Began 38	Ended 23
Eocene	Began 53	Ended 38
Paleocene	Began 65	Ended 53

The Tertiary Period of Earth's history began about 65 million years ago and ended about 2 million years ago.

1. Which epoch began about 5 million years ago?
    - A Pleistocene
    - B Pliocene
    - C Miocene
    - D 2 Million years ago

2. About how long ago did the Oligocene Epoch end?
    - J Miocene Epoch
    - K Eocene Epoch
    - L 23 million years ago
    - M 38 million years ago

3. About how long did the Tertiary Period of Earth's history last?
    - A 63 million years
    - C 65 million years
    - B 65 million years ago
    - D 67 million years

4. About how many years did the Eocene Epoch last?
    - J 91 years
    - K 15 million years
    - L 53 million years
    - M 91 million years

5. Which epoch of the Tertiary Period lasted for the longest time?
    - A 18 million years
    - B Eocene
    - C Cenozoic
    - D Miocene

Write About It

6. The Cenozoic Era has two periods—the Tertiary Period and the Quaternary Period. We are living in the Quaternary Period. How long has it been going on?

    Solve the problem above, and explain how you reached your solution.

    _____
    _____
    _____
    _____

1. A☐ B☐ C☐ D☐   4. J☐ K☐ L☐ M☐
2. J☐ K☐ L☐ M☐   5. A☐ B☐ C☐ D☐
3. A☐ B☐ C☐ D☐

• Adding and Subtracting Whole Numbers

Writing a Word Equation

Sometimes it is hard to see how the information in a word problem fits together. It may help to represent the information in a different way by writing a word equation.

Example

A large pizza costs $10.25 and a small pizza costs $6.25. Paul bought four small pizzas. How much change did he get from $30?

Step 1: **Look at the problem carefully, and decide what you know and what you don't know.**

Do you know how much money Paul gave? _____

Do you know how much four small pizzas cost? _____

Do you know how much change Paul got? _____

Step 2: **Translate the problem to a word equation.** Use numbers for what you know and phrases for what you don't know.

$30 − Cost of the pizzas = Paul's change

Step 3: **To solve the word equation, find the cost of the pizzas.**

How many pizzas did Paul buy? _____

How much did each pizza cost? _____

Number of pizzas x Cost per pizza = Cost of the pizzas

4   x $6.25   =   _____

Step 4: **Now solve the word equation.**

$30   −   Cost of the pizzas   =   Paul's change

$30   −   _____   =   Paul's change

           _____   =   Paul's change

So, Paul got _____ change.

• Dividing Whole Numbers and Money

GUIDED PRACTICE

Find the answer to the word equation for each problem. Then write the answer to the original word problem in a sentence.

1. It costs $15.00 to rent a canoe, plus an extra $2.50 for each hour the canoe is used. How much will it cost to rent a canoe for 3 hours?

   a. Write a word equation.

   $15 + Cost for 3 hours = Total cost

   b. To solve the equation, find the cost for 3 hours.

   3   x   Cost per hour   =   Cost for 3 hours

   3   x   _____   =   _____

   c. Solve the equation.

   $15   + Cost for 3 hours = Total cost

   $15   +   _____   =   _____

   So, it costs _____ to rent a canoe for 3 hours.

2. Sal bought 5 notebooks. He paid $20.00 and received $6.50 in change. How much did each notebook cost?

   a. Write a word equation.

   Total cost ÷ 5 = Cost per notebook

   b. To solve the equation, find the total cost.

   $20.00   —Change Given   =   Total Cost

   $20.00   —   _____   =   _____

   c. Solve the equation.

   Total cost ÷ 5 = Cost per notebook

   _____ ÷ 5 = _____

   So, each notebook cost _____.

Solving Multi-Step Problems

Sometimes it takes several steps to solve a problem. It can be helpful to list the questions you need to answer. Then decide which question you can answer first.

Example

The Parks Department estimated that a new trail would cost $200,000 for labor and $100,000 for materials. The actual cost was $150,495 for labor and $122,384 for materials. What was the difference between the estimated cost and the actual cost?

A. Make a list of the questions you need to answer to solve the problem.

What is the total estimated cost?

What is the total actual cost?

What was the difference between the estimated cost and the actual cost?

B. Look at the list of questions. Decide which question you can answer first.

You can find the estimated cost for labor and materials. You can also find the actual cost for labor and materials.

C. Calculate.

estimated cost of labor and materials
$ 200,000
+ 100,000
$ 300,000

actual cost of labor and materials
$ 150,495
+ 122,384
$ 272,879

D. Write an equation to solve the third question.

Estimated cost – Actual cost = Difference

$300,000 – $272,879 = $ _____

So, the difference between the estimated cost and the

actual cost was $ _____.

• Multiplying Whole Numbers

GUIDED PRACTICE

1. A new building needs 2,050 square yards of indoor carpet and 900 square yards of outdoor carpet. What will the total cost for the carpet be?

Carpet

Type	Cost per square yard
Indoor	$9
Outdoor	$15

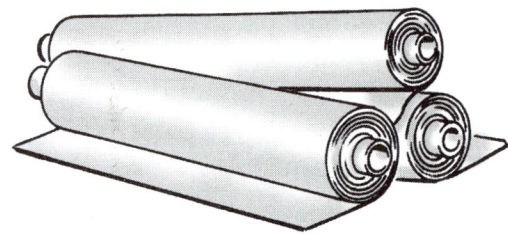

Step 1: Circle the questions you need to answer to solve the problem.

What is the cost of the indoor carpet?

What is the cost of the outdoor carpet?

What will the cost of all the carpeting be?

How many yards of carpeting are needed in all?

Step 2: Decide which question or questions to answer first.

You can find the cost of _____ and the

cost of _____.

Step 3: Calculate.

Cost of indoor carpet = _____ x $ _____ x $ _____

Cost of outdoor carpet = _____ x $ _____ = $ _____

Step 4: Write an equation to solve the problem.

Cost of indoor carpet + Cost of outdoor carpet = Total cost

_____ + _____ = $ _____

So, the total cost for the new carpet will be $ _____.

Chapter 2 **L3**

Making a Table to Generalize

Some problems may ask you to write information as an **expression**, a mathematical phrase. In expressions such as 7 x 18, both numbers are known. Other expressions include an unknown number, a **variable**. Showing information in a table can help you solve problems with variables.

Example 1

Rafael ran n laps every day for 7 days. How many laps did he run?

A. To write an expression, you must decide what operation to use. It can help to substitute numbers for the variable. Make a table supposing Rafael ran 1 lap every day, 12 laps every day, and 5 laps every day.

Laps run per day	Laps run in a week
1	7 (multiply by 7)
12	84
5	

B. Look at the table. The operation you used was multiplication.

In the table you substituted numbers for the variable, n. Now substitute n for the numbers in the table to find the expression.

Laps run per day	Laps run in a week
n	7 x n

So, Rafael ran 7x n laps.

Example 2

A seal eats f pounds of fish each week. How many pounds of fish do 2 seals eat per day?

To decide which operations to use, substitute numbers for the variable and make a table. When you understand the operations being used substitute the variable.

Pounds that 1 seal eats in one week	Pounds that 1 seal eats in one day	Pounds that 2 seals eat in one day
1	1/7 (divide by 7)	2/7 (multiply by 2)
35		
f	$f/7$	x $f/7$

So, 2 seals will eat _____ pounds of fish per week.

• Order of Operations

GUIDED PRACTICE

1. Roberta took *a* apples to the picnic. People ate 25 of the apples. How many apples does Roberta have left?

   To decide what operation to use, substitute numbers for the variable and make a table.

Apples taken to the picnic	Apples left
50	25 (subtract 25)
40	15
31	
a	

   So, Roberta had _____ apples left.

2. Veronica rides her bike to the store. The store is *m* miles from her house. She then rides to the post office which is 2 miles farther. From the post office she rides back home. How many miles does she ride?

   To decide which operations to use, substitute numbers for the variable and make a table.

Miles from house to store	Miles from to	Total miles
1	(add 2)	6 ( )
3		
m	m + 2	

   So, Veronica rides _____ miles.

3. Three friends each take *c* cans of food to the food drive. The cans are distributed equally to 4 families. How many cans does each family receive?

Cans of food from each friend	Total cans brought	
8		
4		
c		

   So, each family receives _____ cans.

PRACTICE

Make a table substituting numbers for the variable.

4. A scientist released 80 birds in a park. If each bird laid *e* eggs, how many eggs would there be?

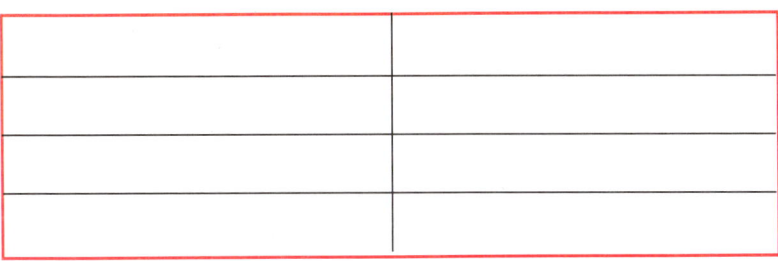

So, there are _____ eggs.

Solve

5. Fleur received $20 for mowing the lawn. She bought two movie tickets for *t* dollars each. How much money does she have left?

6. Mrs. Fitzgerald collected *d* dollars for the fund drive. Her students collected $89. How much money was collected for the fund drive?

7. David has a bag of 16 potatoes. He eats *p* potatoes each day. How many days will David's bag of potatoes last?

8. Each loaf of bread has 15 slices. A baker makes *b* loaves of bread. If 20 loaves do not get sliced, how many slices of bread will the baker have?

9. Alan lifts weights. Last month he could lift *p* pounds. This month he can lift 5 pounds more. How many pounds can Alan lift this month?

10. Xena has 20 cassettes that each cost *m* dollars. She also has 25 CDs that each cost $2 more than a cassette. How much did Xena's CDs cost in all?

• Order of Operations

TEST-TAKING PRACTICE

Choose the best answer for each problem. In the answer section at the bottom of this page, fill in the box of your choice.

1. Each hour, n inches of snow fell. Which operation would you use to find how much snow fell in 8 hours?
   A Add n to 8
   B Subtract n from 8
   C Multiply n by 8
   D Divide n by 8

2. Cal played in a total of 300 baseball games. If he played for y years, how many games did he play on the average each year?
   J $y + 300$
   K $y - 300$
   L $300 \times y$
   M $300 \div y$

3. A basket of fruit has g Golden Delicious apples. It also has 7 fewer Macintosh apples than Golden Delicious. How many apples are in the basket?
   A $g + 7$
   B $g - 7$
   C $(2 \times g) - 7$
   D $(2 \times g) + 7$

4. Together, 2 bags of flour weigh p pounds. If a cook uses 3 pounds from one of the bags, how much flour is left in that bag?
   J $(2 \times p) - 3$
   K $p/2 - 3$
   L $(2 \times p) + 3$
   M $p - 3$

Write About It

5. Angela has a pair of in-line skates with w wheels on each skate. She has a another pair with one less wheel per skate. How many wheels in all are there on Angela's skates?

   Write down a plan for solving the problem. Then solve.

   _____
   _____
   _____
   _____
   _____
   _____
   _____
   _____
   _____
   _____
   _____

1. A ☐ B ☐ C ☐ D ☐
2. J ☐ K ☐ L ☐ M ☐
3. A ☐ B ☐ C ☐ D ☐
4. J ☐ K ☐ L ☐ M ☐

● Order of Operations

Chapter 2 L4

PRACTICE
Use estimation to solve each problem, showing your work.

3. A farmer sells 137 boxes holding 12 eggs each one weekend. Does he meet his target of selling 2,000 eggs?

_____
_____
_____

4. The farmer has 285 heads of lettuce, and packs 22 heads into each crate. Will he need more than 12 crates?

_____
_____
_____

Solve

5. Nate's average score last year was 7.6 points per game. This year, he played in 26 games and scored 286 points. Has his average score improved?

_____

6. Donald sold between 40 and 50 raffle tickets each week. If he sells 1,800 tickets in a month, he wins a prize. Did Donald win a prize?

_____

7. Students sold 521 raffle tickets in a week. If they continue to sell tickets at this rate, will they sell 1,800 tickets in a month?

_____

8. Raquel has $400 to spend on CDs for her music club. Does she have enough money to buy buy 38 CDs that cost $12.00 each?

_____

9. A gardener counts 183 seeds in 1 pack of carrot seeds. Should there be at least 5,000 seeds in 22 packs?

_____

10. Caleb spent $892 of his monthly earnings of $$1,743. Does he have at least $800 left over?

_____

• Estimating Products and Quotients

TEST-TAKING PRACTICE

Choose the correct answer to each problem. Fill in the answer box of your choice in the section at the bottom of the page.

1. Maura's salary is $53,000 per year. Which expression can be used to estimate the amount that Maura earns each week?
   A $55,000 ÷ 12
   B $50,000 x 12
   C $50,000 ÷ 50
   D $53,000 x 52

2. The 38 members of a club each donated $55 toward new furniture. Which expression can best be used to estimate the amount raised toward furniture?
   J   40 x $50
   K   40 x $60
   L $55 ÷ 35
   M $50 ÷ 40

3. A woman walking across the United States covers an average of 22 miles each day. About how many days will it take her to travel 2,310 miles?
   A   about 22 days
   B   about 100 days
   C   about 200 days
   D   about 220 days

4. A scientist counts 178 songbirds in an acre of forest. About how many songbirds would you expect there to be in 320 acres of the forest?
   J   about 500 songbirds
   K   about 5,000 songbirds
   L   about 6,000 songbirds
   M   about 60,000 songbirds

5. Each worker at a steel factory gets paid $182 per day. If there are 315 workers, how much does it cost to run the factory for one day?
   A   about $30,000
   B   about $60,000
   C   about $70,000
   D   Not given

Write About It

6. John wanted to buy 22 feet of lumber that cost $2.10 per foot. He rounded the amounts to 20 feet and $2.00, and took $40 with him to buy the lumber.

   Did John had enough money for the lumber? Explain your answer.

   _____
   _____
   _____
   _____
   _____

1. A☐ B☐ C☐ D☐
2. J☐ K☐ L☐ M☐
3. A☐ B☐ C☐ D☐
4. J☐ K☐ L☐ M☐
5. A☐ B☐ C☐ D☐

• Estimating Products and Quotients

Chapters 1—2

Test-Taking Skill: Writing a Plan

On some tests you need to explain how to solve a problem. It is important to explain your thinking and show your calculations.

Example

A contractor estimated that a new house would cost $80,000 for labor and $100,000 for materials. The actual cost was $89,900 for labor and $102,410 for materials. What was the difference between the estimated cost and the actual cost?

A. Read the problem carefully. Decide what kind answer you are looking for.

The answer that is asked for is an amount of money—the difference between the estimated cost and the actual cost of a new house.

B. Make a plan. Write your plan.

First, find out how much the estimated cost was. Add the amounts estimated for labor and materials. Then find out how much the actual cost was. Add the amounts for labor and materials. Finally, subtract the lesser amount from the greater amount to find the difference.

Here's a shorter way to write the plan.

Step 1: Estimated cost = labor estimate + materials estimate

Step 2: Actual cost = actual labor + actual materials

Step 3: Difference = Actual cost – Estimated cost

C. Solve the problem.

Step 1: Estimated cost: $80,000 + $100,000 = $180,000

Step 2: Actual cost: $89,900 + $102,410 = $192,310

Step 3: Difference: $192,310 – $180,000 = $12,310

D. Remember to answer the question in the problem.

The difference between the estimated and actual cost is _____.

• Test-Taking Skill

TEST-TAKING PRACTICE

Make a plan to solve the problem. Then solve. Explain your thinking. Use the table to find the information you need.

Cost of Building a Deck

Size of deck	15 ft x 15 ft	15 ft x 30 ft	20 ft x 30 ft
Lumber	$2,125	$3,450	$4,445
Labor	$1,450	$1,900	$2,200

1. What is the difference between the cost of building a deck that is 15 ft x 15 ft and building a deck that is 15 ft x 30 ft?

2. A contractor is building one 20 ft x 30 ft deck and two 15 ft x 15 ft decks. What will the cost of the three decks be?

Chapter 3 L1

Writing a Word Equation

If you aren't sure how to start solving a problem, it may help to show the information another way. Write a word equation about what the problem asks.

Example

At the grocery store, Boris bought some lemons for 23 cents each and a tomato for 79 cents. The total cost was $2.17. How many lemons did Boris buy?

A. Make sure you know what the problem asks.

   THINK: The problem asks *how many lemons* Boris bought.

   Find what else you know about the lemons.

   THINK: Each lemon cost $0.23.

B. Write a word equation that includes what you need to find.

   Number of lemons x Cost of one lemon = Total cost of lemons

   or, *Number of lemons* = Total cost of lemons ÷ Cost of one lemon

   Number of lemons   =   ?   ÷ $0.23

   To solve, you need to know the total cost of the lemons.

C. Write an equation to find the total cost of the lemons.

   Total cost of lemons   =   Total cost   −   Cost of tomato

   Total cost of lemons   = $ _____   − $ _____

   Total cost of lemons   = $ _____

D. Substitute what you have found into your first equation.

   Number of lemons   =   Total cost of lemons ÷ Cost of one lemon

   Number of lemons   = $ _____   ÷ $0.23

   Number of lemons   =   _____

   So, Boris bought _____ lemons.

• Dividing by Decimals

GUIDED PRACTICE

1. Monica went to a store to buy clothes. She bought 5 pairs of socks for $4.35 each and one sweater. The total amount of money she spent was $46.70. What was the price of the sweater?

   Step 1: Write a word equation for the price of the sweater.

   Price of sweater = Total cost − Total cost of socks

   Price of sweater = $46.70 − ?

   To solve, you need to know the total cost of the socks.

   Step 2: Write an equation to find the total cost of the socks.

   Total cost of socks = Number of pairs x Cost per pair

   Total cost of socks = _____ x $ _____

   x = $ _____

   Step 3: Substitute what you have found into your first equation.

   Price of sweater = Total cost − Total cost of socks

   Price of sweater = $ _____ − $ _____ = $ _____

   So, the price of the sweater was $ _____.

2. A class of 32 visited the zoo in two equal groups. One group went to the reptile house, where 7 group members watched the snakes while the rest watched the crocodiles. How many watched the crocodiles?

   Step 1: Write a word equation for the number at the crocodiles.

   Number at crocodiles = Number in group − 7

   Step 2: Write an equation to find the number in the group.

   Number in group = Number in class ÷ Number of groups

   Number in group = _____ ÷ _____

   = _____

   Step 3: Substitute what you have found into your first equation.

   Number at crocodiles = Number in group − 7

   Number at crocodiles = _____ − _____ = _____

   So, _____ people watched the crocodiles.

PRACTICE

Write word equations to solve the problem. Then solve, showing your work.

3. Each week during the summer, about 800 kids come to Space Camp. About 75 of them are from foreign countries. If 8,700 kids from the United States come to space camp over the summer, how many weeks does the program last?

_____

_____

_____

_____

Solve

4. At the space camp store Norman buys several packages of freeze dried ice cream for $3.39 each and a package of spaghetti and meatballs for $5.29. The total cost is $18.85. How many packages of ice cream does Norman buy?

_____

5. Garrett and Meg are flying back from space camp. Each plane ticket costs $275. They also have to spend an extra $14 dollars for each bag they bring. If they spend a total of $606 dollars getting home, how many bags did they bring?

_____

6. A space shuttle spent 192 hours in orbit. If the astronauts spent 6 hours a day sleeping, how many hours in all did they spend sleeping in orbit?

_____

7. A class of 32 visited the space camp. Some of them bought souvenirs for $6.50 each, spending a total of $162.50. How many people in the class did not buy souvenirs?

_____

• Dividing by Decimals

TEST-TAKING PRACTICE

Choose the best answer for each problem. In the answer section at the bottom of this page, fill in the box of your choice.

1. Julia did 25 push-ups and a certain number of sit-ups each day for a month. During the 31 days, Julia did a total of 2,170 exercises. Which word equation could you use to find out how many sit-ups she did a day?
   A Days x 2,170 = Sit-ups
   B Push-ups x Sit-ups = 2,170
   C Push-ups + Sit-ups = 2,170
   D 31 x Situps = 2,170

2. Rise buys 10 pounds of coldcuts for $3.65 a pound and pickles for $2.96 a pound. Her bill is $45.38. How many pounds of pickles did she buy?
   J 2.96 lb
   K 3 lb
   L 3.65 lb
   M 4 lb

3. There are 146 seats for a sold-out play. The producers thought that 60 of the seats would be taken by children, but in fact there were 20 more adults than they expected. How many adults attended the play?
   A 40
   B 86
   C 106
   D 126

4. Billy left at 6:30 A.M. to go fishing near his home. He spent 3 hours and 45 minutes fishing and got home at 11:15 A.M. If it took the same amount of time to travel each way, how long did it take Billy to get home?
   J 15 minutes
   K 30 minutes
   L 45 minutes
   M Not given

Write About It

5. Hair grows about 5 inches a year. Quadruplets (4) who had never had their hair cut had a combined hair length of 120 inches in 1998. Write two equations to find out the year in which they were born.

---

1. A ☐ B ☐ C ☐ D ☐   3. A ☐ B ☐ C ☐ D ☐
2. J ☐ K ☐ L ☐ M ☐   4. J ☐ K ☐ L ☐ M ☐

● Dividing by Decimals

Interpreting Quotients

When the answer to a division problem is not a whole number, you may have to decide what kind of answer you need that will match the question you have been asked.

Each of the following is a possible solution to *51 ÷ 12*, depending on the type of problem.

Whole Number and Remainder	Mixed Number in Simplest Form	Decimal	Rounded Up	Rounded Down
51 ÷ 12 → 4 R 3	51 ÷ 12 = $4\frac{1}{4}$	51 ÷ 12 = 4.25	51 ÷ 12 → 5	51 ÷ 12 → 4

Example 1

Joan cut 12-inch lengths of ribbon from a piece 51 inches long. How many inches of ribbon did she have left over?

Step 1: Read the problem carefully to determine what you are being asked.

The problem asks how many inches of ribbon are left over—so the answer will be a remainder.

Step 2: Divide. Write the answer as a whole number and remainder.

51 ÷ 12 → _____

Step 3: The answer to the problem will be the remainder.

So, Joan will have _____ inches of ribbon left over.

Example 2

Bob cut 51 inches of rope into 12 equal lengths. How long was each piece of rope?

Step 1: Read the problem carefully to determine what you are being asked.

The problem asks for a measurement in <u>inches</u>—so the answer will be a fraction, whole number, or mixed number in simplest form.

Step 2: Divide. Write the answer as a mixed number in simplest form.

51 ÷ 12 = _____

Step 3: Don't forget to include the units in your answer.

So, each piece of rope was _____ inches long.

• Dividing Whole Numbers with Decimal Quotients

GUIDED PRACTICE

Whole Number and Remainder	Mixed Number in Simplest Form	Decimal	Rounded Up	Rounded Down
51 ÷ 12 → 4 R 3	51 ÷ 12 = $4\frac{1}{4}$	51 ÷ 12 = 4.25	51 ÷ 12 → 5	51 ÷ 12 → 4

1. Charles cut 51 meters of rope into 12 equal lengths. How many meters long was each piece of rope?

   a. **Read the problem to determine what you are being asked.**

   The problem asks how many <u>meters</u> long each piece of rope was—so the answer should be written as a whole number or as a decimal.

   b. **Divide, and write the answer as a decimal. Don't forget the units in your answer.**

   51 ÷ 12 = _____

   So, each piece of rope was _____ meters long.

2. A school is renting vans for a field trip. Each van holds 12 students. How many vans will the school need for 51 students?

   a. **Read the problem to determine what you are being asked.**

   The problem asks how many vans are needed—so the answer will be rounded up to a whole number.

   b. **Divide, rounding up to the next whole number.**

   51 ÷ 12 → _____

   So, the school will need _____ vans.

3. Elvira sells the eggs that her chickens lay. She has 51 eggs. How many boxes of eggs can she sell, if each box holds 12 eggs?

   a. **Read the problem to determine what you are being asked.**

   The problem asks how many boxes will be filled—so the answer will be a whole number, rounded down.

   b. **Divide, rounding down to a whole number.**

   51 ÷ 12 → _____

   So, Elvira can sell _____ boxes of eggs.

Chapter 3 | **L2**

PRACTICE

4. Complete the table to show the answer to 52 ÷ 5 in five different ways.

Whole Number and Remainder	Mixed Number in Simplest Form	Decimal	Rounded Up	Rounded Down
52 ÷ 5 →	52 ÷ 5 =	52 ÷ 5 =	52 ÷ 5 →	52 ÷ 5 →

Use the completed chart to answer the problems.

5. Sharon has 52 minutes worth of videotape left on a cassette. How many 5-minute cartoon shows can she record on the tape?

   _____

6. Larry cuts as many 5-inch pieces of wire as he can from a 52-inch roll. How many inches of wire are left over?

   _____

7. Susan divided 52 yards of fabric into 5 equal lengths. How long was each length of fabric?

   _____

8. Art cut 52 centimeters of rope into 5 equal pieces. How long was each piece of rope?

   _____

9. The 5 members of a club shared the expenses equally for a trip that they took together. The total cost of the trip was $52. How much did each member pay?

   _____

10. A restaurant uses 5 ounces of hamburger meat for each burger. If the cook makes hamburger patties from 52 ounces of meat, how many ounces will she have left over?

    _____

11. Eric is renting tables for a party. Each table seats 5 people. How many tables will Eric need if 52 people are expected at the party?

    _____

12. Jorge has a collection of 52 CDs. He is stacking them on a shelf in groups of 5. How many complete stacks can Jorge make?

    _____

• Dividing Whole Numbers with Decimal Quotients

TEST-TAKING PRACTICE

Choose the best answer for each problem. In the answer section at the bottom of this page, fill in the box of your choice.

1. **Tom has a roll of wrapping paper 57 inches long. How many packages can he wrap if he uses 9 inches of paper for each package?**

    A 6.33 packages
    B $6\frac{1}{3}$ packages
    C 6 packages
    D 7 packages

2. **Betty cut a 27-inch ribbon into six equal lengths. How long is each piece of ribbon?**

    J 5 inches
    K $4\frac{1}{2}$ inches
    L 4 inches
    M 4 inches remainder 3

3. **Large picnic tables can seat 12 people each. How many tables would you need to seat a group of 100 people?**

    A $8\frac{1}{3}$ tables   C 10 tables
    B 9 tables   D 11 tables

4. **A box of 12 pens costs $5.52. What is the cost of each pen?**

    J $0.40   L $4.60
    K $0.46   M $5.40

5. **The 16 people at a party ordered 6 large pizzas. If everyone ate the same amount, how many pizzas did each person eat?**

    A $\frac{3}{8}$ pizza   C 1 pizza
    B $\frac{1}{2}$ pizza   D $2\frac{2}{3}$ pizzas

6. **A carpenter is cutting 15-inch shelves from a 72-inch board. How many inches of the board will be left over?**

    J 4 shelves   L 3 inches
    K 5 shelves   M Not given

Write About It

7. **Explain why you can use division to solve the following problem. Can you tell whether any of the boxes have more than 21 books?**

    Wendy packed 86 books in 4 boxes that were different sizes. How many books did she pack into each box?

    _____
    _____
    _____
    _____

1. A ☐ B ☐ C ☐ D ☐   4. J ☐ K ☐ L ☐ M ☐
2. J ☐ K ☐ L ☐ M ☐   5. A ☐ B ☐ C ☐ D ☐
3. A ☐ B ☐ C ☐ D ☐   6. J ☐ K ☐ L ☐ M ☐

● Dividing Whole Numbers with Decimal Quotients

Chapter 3 | **L3**

Using Simpler Numbers

Sometimes a word problem may seem confusing because the numbers you have to use are decimals or fractions. As a first step, rewrite the problem with simpler numbers to decide how to solve the problem.

Example 1

A chemist has 76.5 g of iron filings. How many containers can she fill if each container will hold 4.25 g of iron filings?

Step 1: **Rewrite the problem using simpler numbers.**

A chemist has **80** g of iron filings. How many containers can she fill if each contrainer will hold **4** g of iron filings?

Step 2: **Decide how to solve the problem using the simpler numbers.**
THINK: **I can divide to solve the problem.**

$80 \div 4 = 20$

Step 3: **Now use the actual numbers from the problem.**

$76.5 \div 4.25 = $ _____

So, the chemist can fill _____ containers.

Example 2

A chemist mixed 15.7 g of sulfur, 10.6 g of charcoal, and 3.8 g of salt. She divided the mixture into 7 equal parts. How much did each part weigh?

Step 1: **Rewrite the problem using simpler numbers.**

A chemist mixed 15 g of sulfur, 10 g of charcoal, and 3 g of salt. She divided the mixture into 7 equal parts. How much did each part weigh?

Step 2: **Decide how to solve the problem using the simpler numbers.**
THINK: **I can divide the total number of grams by the number of parts.**

Total grams = $15 + 10 + 3 = 28$

$28 \div 7 = 4$

Step 3: **Now use the actual numbers from the problem.**

Total grams = $15.7 + 10.6 + 3.8 = $ _____

_____ $\div 7 = $ _____

So, each part weighs _____ grams.

• Dividing by Whole Numbers and Decimals

GUIDED PRACTICE

1. How many 1.8 m lengths of wood molding does Enrique need to cover a distance of 28.8 m?

   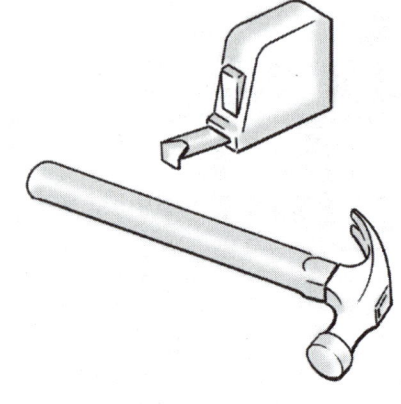

   a. **Rewrite the problem using simpler numbers.**

   How many **2** m lengths of wood molding does Enrique need to cover a distance of **28** m?

   b. **Divide to solve the problem using the simpler numbers.**

   28 ÷ 2 = _____

   c. **Solve, using the actual numbers from the problem.**

   28.8 ÷ 1.8 = _____

   So, Enrique needs _____ lengths of molding.

2. At the store, Naima spends exactly $20. She spends $7.32 on dried fruit, and also buys 10.1 kg of flour. How much does the flour cost per kilogram?

   a. **Rewrite the decimal amounts using simpler numbers.**

   Naima spends _____ on dried fruit, and also buys _____ kg of flour.

   b. **Decide how to solve the problem using the simpler numbers.**
   THINK: I can divide the cost of the flour by its weight in kg.

   Cost of the flour = $20 – $7 = $13

   13 ÷ 10 = _____

   c. **Solve, using the actual numbers from the problem.**

   $20.00 – $7.32 = _____

   _____ ÷ 10.1 = _____

   So, the flour costs $ _____ per kilogram.

Chapter 3 L3

PRACTICE
Solve. Use simpler numbers if you need help deciding where to start.

3. Penny works for 26 hours one week, and earns $165.10 in pay. How much does she earn per hour?

4. Camilla buys 6 stickers for $0.18 each and 3 erasers for $0.35 each. How much does she spend in all?

5. Ray added $1.45 liters of water to 0.53 liters of concentrate. He then poured the mixture equally into 3 containers. How many liters of mixture did each container hold?

6. Angel is driving the 31.85 km from his house to his mother's house. He has driven 19.9 km of the way when his car gets a flat tire. How far is he from his mother's house?

7. If a tablecloth costs $12.65 and a placemat costs $3.45, how much will 2 tablecloths and 8 placemats cost?

8. A rectangular room has an area of 29.14 sq m. If the room is 4.7 m wide, how long is it?

9. Meg's puppy doubled its weight during its first month of life, and then became 2.71 kg heavier. If the puppy nows weighs 8.83 kg, what did it weigh at birth?

10. Steve and Rick shared the cost of an afternoon on the river. In all, they paid $20.75 for canoe rental, $5.40 for lifejackets, and $6.91 for a picnic lunch. How much did each pay?

• Dividing by Whole Numbers and Decimals

TEST-TAKING PRACTICE

Choose the best answer for each problem. In the answer section at the bottom of this page, fill in the box of your choice.

1. Keiko's car traveled 91 km on 5.2 liters of gasoline. How many kilometers did her car travel per liter of gasoline?
   - A 17.5 l
   - B 17.5 km
   - C 18 km
   - D 85.8 km

2. Ginny and Rose each bought a CD that cost $12.65 and a casette that cost $8.49. How much did they pay in all?
   - J $10.57
   - K $21.14
   - L $42.28
   - M $84.56

3. Kerry has 59.2 meters of electrical wire that she cuts into 1.6 meter-lengths. How many lengths of wire does Kerry have?
   - A 4 lengths
   - B 16 lengths
   - C 30 lengths
   - D 37 lengths

4. A box of 12 birthday cards costs $7.68, and a first-class stamp costs $0.33. How much will it cost for a birthday card and the stamp?
   - J $0.31
   - K $0.64
   - L $0.97
   - M $1.10

5. At a store, a sweater costs $22.45 and a shirt costs $17.99. How much more expensive than the shirt is the sweater?
   - A $3.46
   - B $4.46
   - C $20.22
   - D Not Given

6. Sean, Alex, Africa, and Lars shared equally the cost of a taxi ride that came to $13.44. How much did each person pay?
   - J $3.36
   - K $4.48
   - L $6.72
   - M $13.44

Write About It

7. Choose simpler numbers for the following problem, and show the steps you take to solve the problem.

   The length of a field is 18.4 m. The room's area is 252.08 sq m. What is the width of the field?

---

1. A ☐ B ☐ C ☐ D ☐
2. J ☐ K ☐ L ☐ M ☐
3. A ☐ B ☐ C ☐ D ☐
4. J ☐ K ☐ L ☐ M ☐
5. A ☐ B ☐ C ☐ D ☐
6. J ☐ K ☐ L ☐ M ☐

• Dividing by Whole Numbers and Decimals

Chapter 3 | L4

Solving a Missing Factor Problem

Some problems present a product and one of its factors, and ask you to find the missing factor. Because multiplication and division are related operations, you can solve these problems by representing the information in a different way.

Example 1

A barrel floating down a river travels at a rate of 2.5 miles per hour. How long will the barrel take to travel 17.5 miles?

Step 1: Find the relationship among the numbers.

THINK: I can multiply the barrel's speed by the time it takes to find the distance.

$2.5 \times t = 17.5$

Step 2: Rewrite the equation as a division problem.

$17.5 \div 2.5 = t$

$t = 5$

So, it takes _____ hours for the barrel to travel 17.5 miles.

> Remember that multiplication and division are related.

Example 2

The members of a band march in equal rows of 7 people each. All together, there are 98 people in the band. How many people are in each row?

Step 1: Find the relationship among the numbers.

THINK: I can multiply the number of rows by the number in each row to find the total number of people.

$7 \times n = 98$

Step 2: Rewrite the equation as a division problem.

$98 \div 7 = n$

$n = 14$

So, there are _____ people in each row.

• Dividing by Whole Numbers and Decimals

GUIDED PRACTICE

1. Each table at a restaurant has 5 chairs, and each chair weighs 3.6 kg. The chairs were shipped from Italy, and the total weight was 378 kg. How many tables are there at the restaurant?

   a. **Find the relationship among the numbers.**

   THINK: The product of the weight of each chair, the number of chairs per table, and the number of tables will equal the total weight of the shipment.

   $3.6 \times 5 \times n = 378$

   So, $18 \times n = 378$

   b. **Rewrite the equation as a division problem.**

   $378 \div \underline{\qquad} = n$

   $n = \underline{\qquad}$

   So, there are _____ tables at the restaurant.

2. The volume of a box is 1,414 cubic centimeters. The box's length is 20.2 cm, and its height is 14 cm. What is the width of the box?

   a. **Find the relationship among the numbers.**

   THINK: The volume of the box is the product of its length, width, and height. $V = l \times h \times w$

   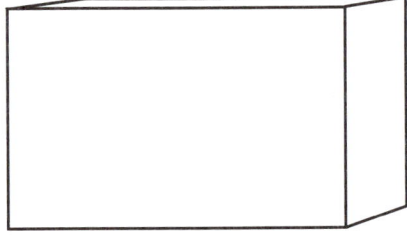

   $1{,}414 = 20.2 \times 14 \times w$

   So, $1{,}414 = 282.8 \times w$

   b. **Rewrite the equation as a division problem.**

   $\underline{\qquad} \div \underline{\qquad} = w$

   $w = \underline{\qquad}$

   So, the height of the box is _____ cm.

Chapter 3 | **L4**

PRACTICE

Write an equation for each problem. Then find the missing factor to solve the problem.

3. The width of a rectangular room is 3.75 m and its area is 22.5 sq m. What is the length of the room?

4. A train moving at a constant speed travels for 3.5 hours and covers 280 km. What is its speed?

5. Jo is cooking fish for a party. She buys 0.4 pounds of fish per person, and pays a total of $26.70. The fish sells for $4.45 per pound. How many servings is Jo making?

6. A houseware store takes in $264 one day from the sale of 20 sets of dinner plates. Each set consists of 6 plates. What is the price of a single dinner plate?

7. One week, Regina buys a tunafish sandwich for lunch each schoolday. She spends $11.50 on the sandwiches. How much does each tunafish sandwich cost?

8. An elevator is loaded with 12 identical crates, which together weigh 990 kg, the maximum weight the elevator can carry. How much does each crate weigh?

● Dividing by Whole Numbers and Decimals

TEST-TAKING PRACTICE

Choose the equation that can be used to find the missing factor. Fill in the answer box of your choice in the section at the bottom of the page.

1. A hiker is walking at a speed of 3.5 miles per hour. How many hours, t, will it take him to travel 14 miles?
   A $3.5 \div t = 14$
   B $t \div 3.5 = 14$
   C $14 \times 3.5 = t$
   D $3.5 \times t = 14$

2. The volume of a cube is 216 cubic feet. What is the length l of each side of the cube?
   J $l \times l = 216$
   K $l \times l \times l = 216$
   L $l + l + l = 216$
   M Not given

3. Riva bought several necklaces that each cost $6.35. She spent a total of $44.45. How many necklaces, n, did Riva buy?
   A $n = 6.35 \times 44.45$
   B $n \div 6.35 = 44.45$
   C $n = 44.45 \div 6.35$
   D $n \times 44.45 = 6.35$

4. Peter and Penny purchased 3 pies a piece and paid the person a total of $4. What was the price, p, per pie?
   J $4 = 2 \times 3 \times p$
   K $3 = 2 \times 4 \times p$
   L $2 = 3 \times 4 \times p$
   M $p = 2 \times 3 \times 4$

Write an equation, then solve each problem. Fill in the answer box of your choice in the section at the bottom of the page.

5. The length of a box is 1.4 m, and its width is 0.8 m. If the box has a volume of 4.48 cu m, what is its height?
   A 3.2 m
   B 4 m
   C 5 m
   D 5.6 m

6. Claudia gives her son $2.75 each week. If she has given him $170.50 so far, how many weeks have gone by?
   J 56 weeks
   K 62 weeks
   L 172 weeks
   M 469 weeks

Write About It

7. At a track meet, each team member pays $4.00. There are 8 teams, and a total of $320 is collected. How many members are there on each team? Write the problem as an equation using multiplication, and then as an equation using division. Solve the equation.

   _____

   _____

   _____

   _____

   _____

1. A☐ B☐ C☐ D☐   4. J☐ K☐ L☐ M☐
2. J☐ K☐ L☐ M☐   5. A☐ B☐ C☐ D☐
3. A☐ B☐ C☐ D☐   6. J☐ K☐ L☐ M☐

• Dividing by Whole Numbers and Decimals

Underlining Needed Information

Problems with tables usually include more information than you need. The example shows how to underline the needed information in both the problem and the table.

Example

Cathy collects small china animals. She keeps the collection on four shelves. The top shelf holds <u>3 cats</u> and <u><u>all the spiders</u></u>. Cathy wants to put a felt pad on the end of each leg. How many legs do the animals on the top shelf have?

China Animals on Cathy's Shelves

Animal	Number of Animals	Number of Legs
Fish	6	0
Owls	5	2
Cats	<u>3</u>	<u>4</u>
Spiders	<u><u>6</u></u>	<u><u>8</u></u>

Step 1: Mark related information in the same way to help you keep track of it. Information about the cats is underlined once; information about the spiders is underlined twice.

Step 2: Use the information that you underlined to write a word equation. Then, fill in the numbers you know.

Number of cats' legs + **Number of spiders' legs** = **Total legs**

↓ ↓ ↓

3 cats with 4 legs each + **6 spiders with 8 legs each** = **?**

Step 3: Write a number equation. Then, solve.

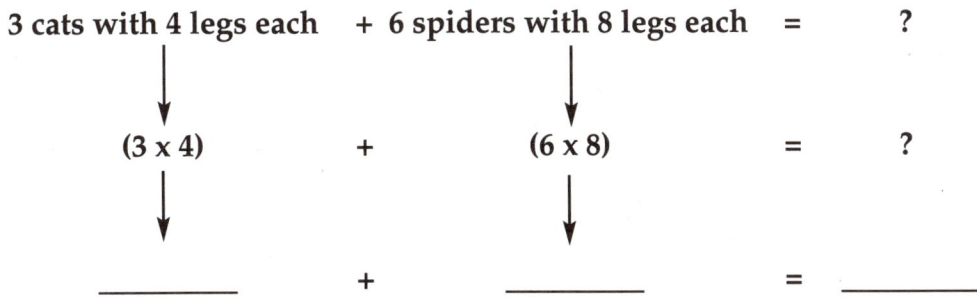

So, the animals on the top shelf have _____ legs.

• Multiplying Whole Numbers

GUIDED PRACTICE

Use the table to solve each problem.

1. Ms. Chang drove from Scottston to Centerville. Then, she drove from Centerville to North Bluff. How far did she drive?

   Step 1: Underline the information you need in the problem and the table.

   Step 2: Write a word equation and a number equation for the problem. Then, solve.

Distance from Centerville to Other Towns

Town	Distance (in miles)
Scottston	37 mi
West Bend	126 mi
North Bluff	84 mi
Hartsburg	55 mi

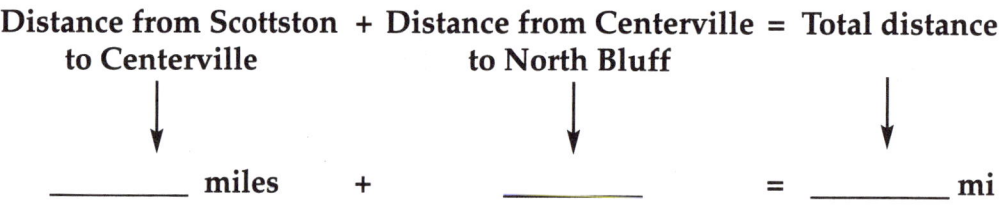

_____ miles   +   _____   =   _____ mi

So, Ms. Chang drove _____ miles.

2. Mr. Guzik drove from Centerville to West Bend and back to Centerville. Then, he drove to Hartsburg. How far did he drive?

   Step 1: Underline the information you need in the problem and the table.

   Step 2: Write a word equation and a number equation for the problem. Then, solve.

Distance from Centerville to Other Towns

Town	Distance (in miles)
Scottston	37 mi
West Bend	126 mi
North Bluff	84 mi
Hartsburg	55 mi

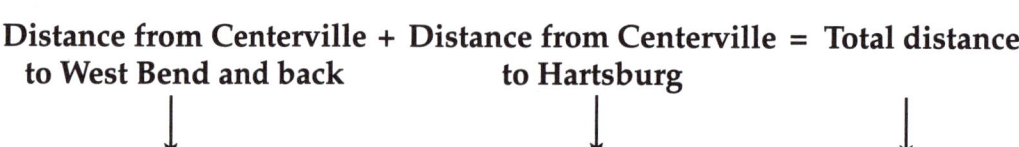

2 x _____ miles   +   _____   =   _____ mi

So, Mr. Guzik drove _____ miles.

PRACTICE

Underline important information that you need in the problem and in the table. Write word and number equations to explain the problem. Then, solve.

3. Jerry is selling seed packets to raise money for the Environmental Club. The club will receive the amounts shown in the table for each packet sold. Jerry sold a total of 48 seed packets. He sold 8 packets of peas and 2 packets of spinach. **How much did the club receive for the peas and the spinach?**

Amount Received Per Packet

Seed	1–4 Packets Sold	5 or More Packets Sold
Peas	25¢	30¢
Carrots	22¢	28¢
Spinach	20¢	24¢
Onions	24¢	30¢

_____

_____

_____

4. As part of an experiment, Renata counted all the vowels in the sentences in this problem. She found 50 vowels. **How many of those vowels were *not* either an *a* or an *e*?**

Vowels Found in Problem 4

Vowel	Number
A	10
E	21
I	5
O	12
U	2

_____

_____

_____

_____

• Multiplying Whole Numbers

TEST-TAKING PRACTICE

Choose the best answer for each problem. In the answer section at the bottom of the page, fill in the box of your choice.

Use the information and table below for Problems 1—5.

The Pioneers: High Scores

Player	Goals in Game 1	Goals in Game 2
Irene	2	0
Natasha	1	3
Elizabeth	3	1
Kellene	4	2
Grace	0	3

1. Which information do you need to find how many goals the high scorers made in Game 1?
   - A number of goals scored by Irene, Natasha, and Grace in Game 1
   - B number of goals scored in Game 2
   - C number of players on the team
   - D number of goals scored by Irene, Natasha, Elizabeth, and Kellene in Game 1

2. Natasha's sister, also a Pioneer, scored as many goals as Natasha in the first two games. Who is Natasha's sister?
   - J Irene
   - K Kellene
   - L Elizabeth
   - M Grace

3. The tallest player on the team scored 3 fewer goals than the Pioneers' highest scorer. Who is the tallest player?
   - A Irene
   - B Natasha
   - C Kellene
   - D Grace

4. Natasha and Grace can't come to Game 3. Who will be the highest scoring Pioneer at the game?
   - J Irene
   - K Elizabeth
   - L Kellene
   - M Not given

Write About It
Write a plan for solving the following problem. Sample answer given.

5. During Game 3, Sylvia scored 2 goals. What information do you need to decide whether Sylvia should be listed in the High Scorers table now?

   _____
   _____
   _____
   _____
   _____
   _____
   _____

---

1. A ☐ B ☐ C ☐ D ☐   3. A ☐ B ☐ C ☐ D ☐
2. J ☐ K ☐ L ☐ M ☐   4. J ☐ K ☐ L ☐ M ☐

• Multiplying Whole Numbers

Interpreting Changes in a Line Graph

Sometimes, the information you need to solve a problem is in a line graph.

The direction and steepness of the line connecting the points in a line graph can provide information you need to solve a problem.

- A horizontal line shows no change.
- A line sloping upward shows an increase.
- A line sloping downward shows a decrease.

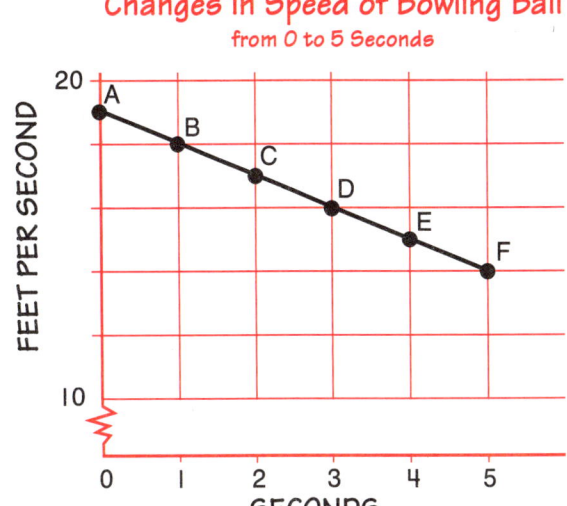

Example 1
What was the speed of the bowling ball 2 seconds after it was rolled?

A. Find the value of each interval on the vertical axis.

Use a finger to count the number of intervals between 10 and 20.

Divide the range, which is 10, by the number of intervals.

10 ÷ _____ = _____. So, each interval represents 2 feet per sec.

B. Look for the point plotted directly above 2 seconds on the horizontal axis.

If the point is between two grid lines, write the values of both.

Which values is the point halfway between?

_____ ft per sec and _____ ft per sec

So, the speed of the bowling ball at 2 seconds was _____ ft per sec.

Example 2
Did the speed of the bowling ball increase or decrease in the time shown?

Look at the slope of the line.

The line slopes downward. So, the speed _____.

• Subtracting Whole Numbers

GUIDED PRACTICE

Use the line graph below to find the information you need to solve the problems.

The graph shows the altitude of Marian's sled as she takes it up a hill and then rides it back down.

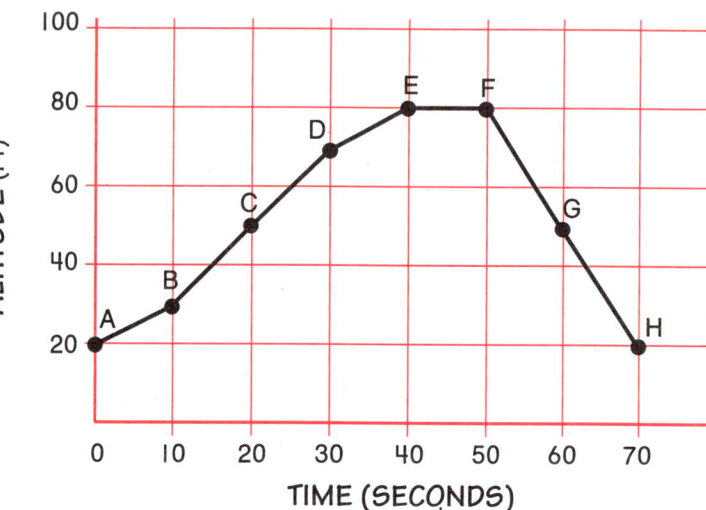

Change in Altitude of Marian's Sled

1. When was Marian's sled the highest?

   a. **Look for the two highest points on the graph.**

   The two highest points are Points _____ and _____.

   b. **Run your finger from each of the two points to the horizontal axis.**

   What times do Points E and F correspond to on the horizontal axis?

   _____ seconds and _____ seconds

   > The steepness of a line can tell you how fast the change is over a time interval. The steeper the line, the faster the change.

   So, Marian's sled was highest at _____ seconds and _____ seconds.

2. Between which two points was Marian's sled traveling the fastest—between Points A and E, or between Points F and H?

   Look at the line between Points A and E. Compare it to the line between Points F and H.

   Which line is steeper? _____

   So, Marian's sled was traveling the fastest between Points _____.

3. When did the sled finish the sled run?

   a. **Find the last point on the graph.**

   The last point is point _____.

   b. **Find the corresponding time.** _____ seconds

   So, the sled finished the sled run at _____.

56

Chapter 4 | L2

PRACTICE

Use the line graph to find the information you need to solve the problems.
The graph shows the change in temperature on one day in April.

4. What was the temperature at 8 A.M.?

   _____

5. At what time was the temperature the lowest?

   When was it the highest?

   _____

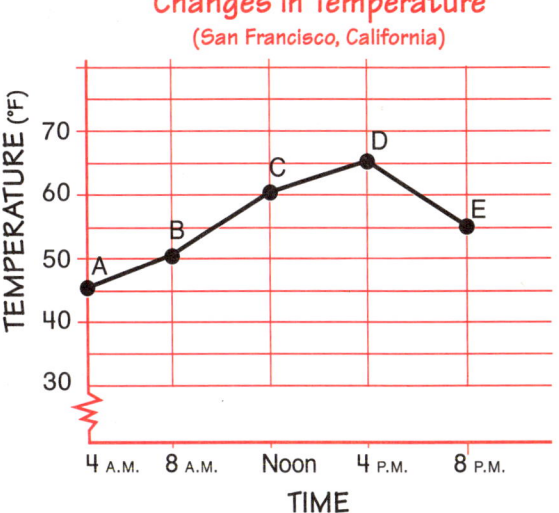

6. Between what times did the temperature increase?

   _____

7. Between which two points did the temperature increase by 10°?

   _____

Solve

8. At which times was the temperature greater than 50 degrees?

   _____

9. Between which two points did the temperature decrease? How much did it decrease?

   _____

10. How much higher was the temperature at 4 P.M. than at 4 A.M.?

    _____

11. Between what times did the temperature change the fastest?

    _____

• Subtracting Whole Numbers

TEST-TAKING PRACTICE

Choose the best answer for each problem. In the answer section at the bottom of this page, fill in the box of your choice.

Use the graph below for Problems 1–5.

Anne recorded how her puppy's weight changed from birth to 1 year. She put the results in a line graph.

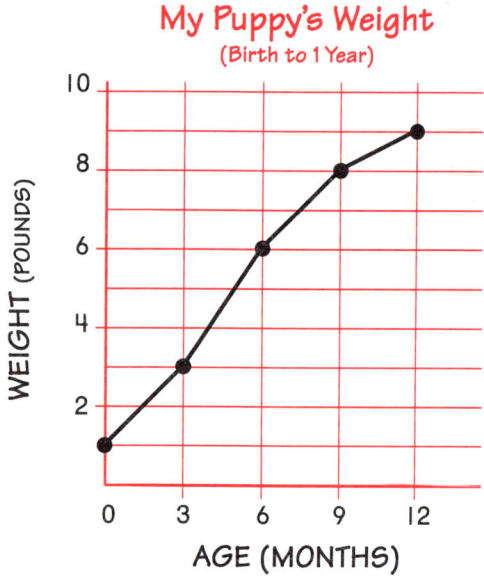

1. What was the puppy's weight at 3 months?
   - A 1 lb
   - B 2 lb
   - C 3 lb
   - D 4 lb

2. Which choice correctly describes the change in the puppy's weight from 0 to 3 months?
   - J an increase from 1 lb to 3 lb
   - K an increase from 2 lb to 3 lb
   - L an increase from 3 lb to 6 lb
   - M a decrease from 3 lb to 1 lb

3. Between which months did the puppy's weight increase the most?
   - A 0–3 months
   - B 3–6 months
   - C 6–9 months
   - D 9–12 months

4. What was the overall change in the puppy's weight from birth to 12 months?
   - J It dropped by 8 pounds.
   - K It increased by 8 pounds.
   - L It increased by 9 pounds.
   - M Not given

Write About It

Write a plan for solving the following problem. Then solve.

5. How could you use the line graph to find how old the puppy was when it reached 8 pounds?

---

1. A☐ B☐ C☐ D☐
2. J☐ K☐ L☐ M☐
3. A☐ B☐ C☐ D☐
4. J☐ K☐ L☐ M☐

58 • Subtracting Whole Numbers

Reading a Double-Bar Graph

A double-bar graph compares related sets of information. The graph below shows the results of a survey, of 100 females and 100 males, on sports activities. It compares the number of males and females who chose each activity.

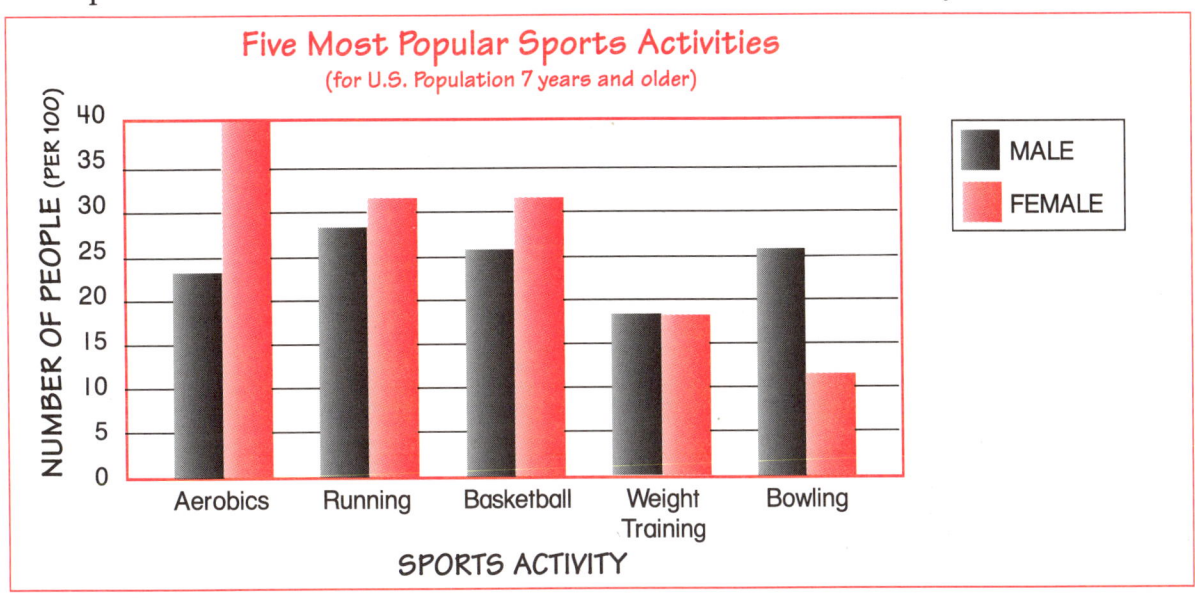

Example 1

How many more females than males chose aerobics?

A. Find the double bar labeled *Aerobics*.

B. The **key** next to the graph tells you what each bar represents.

The black bars show the number of males who chose each activity.

The _____ bars show the number of females who chose each activity.

C. Find the number of males and females who chose aerobics.

If the value lies between grid lines, estimate the amount.

The number of males who chose aerobics is _____.

The number of females who chose aerobics is _____.

D. Subtract to solve.   40 – _____ = _____.

So, about _____ more females than males chose aerobics.

Example 2

Which three sports activities were most popular with males?

The three tallest bars are for running, basketball, and _____.

So, the three sports activities most popular with males were

_____, _____, and _____.

• Subtracting Decimals

59

GUIDED PRACTICE

Use the double-bar graph below to find the information you need to solve the problems. The graph shows how much money you will have after 1 year and after 3 years if you invest $500 in each of the plans shown.

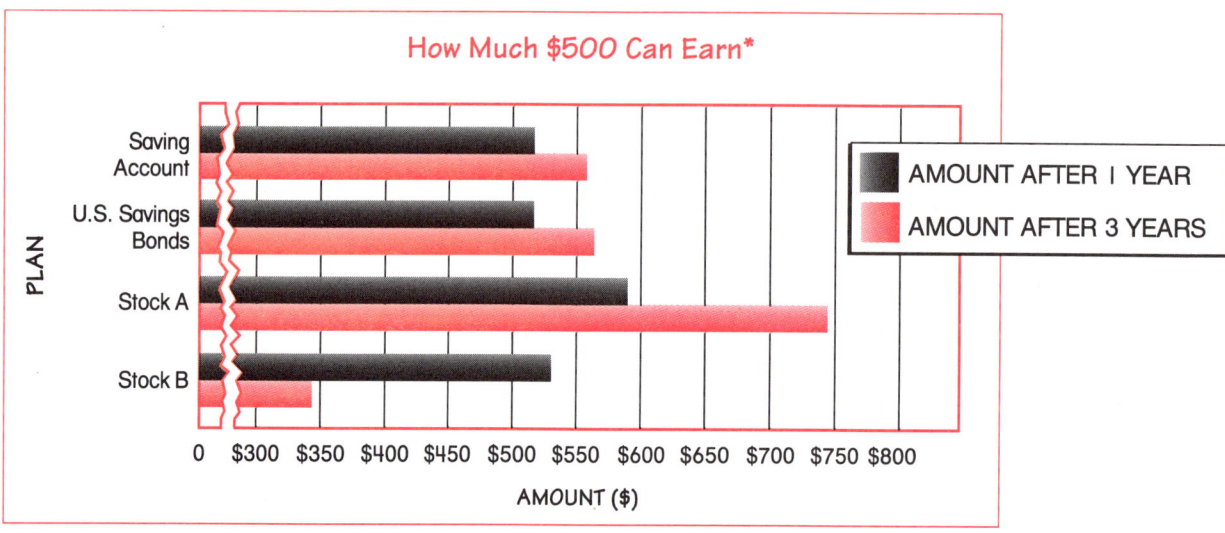

* All amounts are rounded to the nearest $10. Interest rates vary from bank to bank for savings accounts. The savings-account data are based on 4% interest. A stock is a share in a company.

1. Which of the four plans totaled $520 after 1 year?

   a. **Find the bars that show the amount after 1 year.**

   Which color bars show the amount after 1 year? the _____ bars

   b. **Find the bar or bars that show a value of about $520.**

   THINK: The value $520 will be between $500 and $550, but it will be closer to $500.

   Which three black bars are between $500 and $550?

   the _____, _____, and _____ bars

   Which two black bars show about $520?

   the _____ and _____ bars

2. Which plans were worth more than $500 after 3 years?

   a. **Which bars show totals after 3 years?** the _____ bars

   b. **Which three red bars show more than $500?**

   the _____ bar, the _____ bar,

   and the _____ bar

Chapter 4 L3

PRACTICE

Use the double-bar graph to find the information you need to solve the problems.

A scientist tested two people's response times to different sense stimuli such as sounds or smells. The results are shown in the graph below.

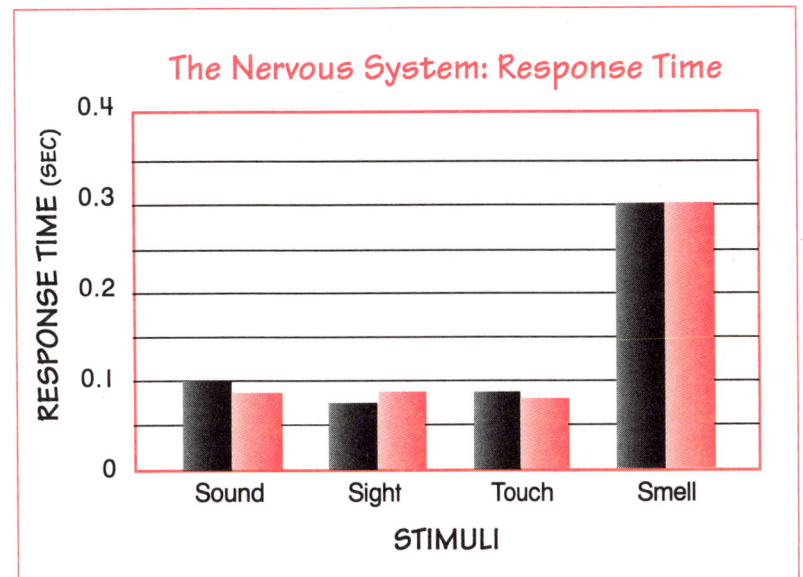

3. On the graph, a shorter bar means a _____ response time.

4. How quick was Jean's response to sight?
   _____

5. How quick was Dale's response to sound?
   _____

6. Who responded more quickly to touch?
   _____

Solve

7. For which stimuli did both people have the same response time?
   _____

8. About how much more quickly did Jean respond to sound than Dale?
   _____

9. To which stimulus did Dale respond the most quickly?
   _____

10. To which one of these four stimuli would you predict most people respond the most slowly?
    _____

• Subtracting Decimals

TEST-TAKING PRACTICE

Choose the best answer for each problem. In the answer section at the bottom of the page, fill in the box of your choice.

Use the graph below for Problems 1–5.

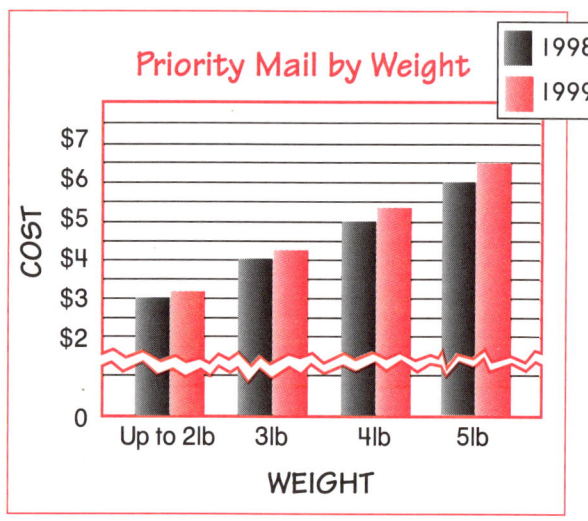

If you send a letter or package by Priority Mail, it will get to most places in 2 days. The graph shows the Priority Mail rates for various weights.

1. Which bars on the graph compare the cost of using Priority Mail to send a 4-lb package?
   A the bars for $4
   B the bars at the far right
   C the two bars labeled 4 lb
   D the black bar labeled 4 lb

2. Which choice describes the change in price for a 2-lb package from 1998 to 1999?
   J an increase from $3.00 to $3.20
   K a decrease from $4.00 to $3.20
   L an increase from $3.00 to $3.50
   M a decrease from $3.20 to $3.00

3. Which weight had the biggest price increase from 1998 to 1999?
   A Up to 2 lb   C 4 lb
   B 3 lb   D 5 lb

4. How much more did it cost to mail a 3-lb package in 1999 than in 1998?
   J $0   L about $0.75
   K about $0.30   M Not given

Write About It
Write a plan for solving the following problem. Then solve.

5. About how much did it cost in 1999 to send a 4-lb package and a 5-lb package by Priority Mail?

_____
_____
_____
_____
_____
_____
_____
_____

1. A☐ B☐ C☐ D☐
2. J☐ K☐ L☐ M☐
3. A☐ B☐ C☐ D☐
4. J☐ K☐ L☐ M☐

Reading a Double Line Graph

A double-line graph compares the ways two related sets of data changed over time. The graph at the right shows how the number of words read per minute by two students changed from first grade to sixth grade.

Example 1

What **trends** does the graph show? Did the words per minute increase, decrease, or stay the same for the time shown?

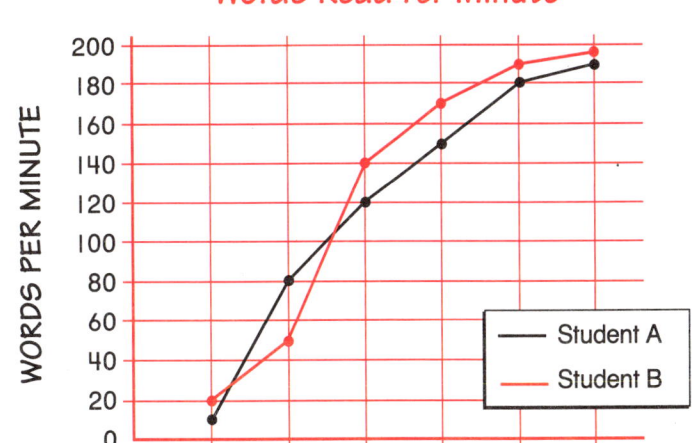

THINK: A *horizontal line* shows **no change**.

A line *sloping upward* shows an **increase**.

A line *sloping downward* shows a **decrease**.

Both lines slope _____.

So, the words read per minute _____ over the time shown.

Example 2

Which student read more words per minute for most of the time shown?

A. Look at the graph of the two lines.

THINK: The numbers on the vertical axis go from 0 to 200 words per minute. So, the student with the higher line read more words per minute.

Which line on the graph is usually higher than the other?

The _____ line is usually higher.

B. Look at the key. Find the student represented by that line.

The student represented by the red line is _____.

So, the student who read more words read per minute for most of the period shown is _____.

• Subtracting Whole Numbers

GUIDED PRACTICE

Use the double-line graph to find the information you need to solve the problems.

The graph shows the price of shares in two mutual funds at the end of each year from 1996–2000. A mutual fund invests money for people, usually by buying stock in other companies.

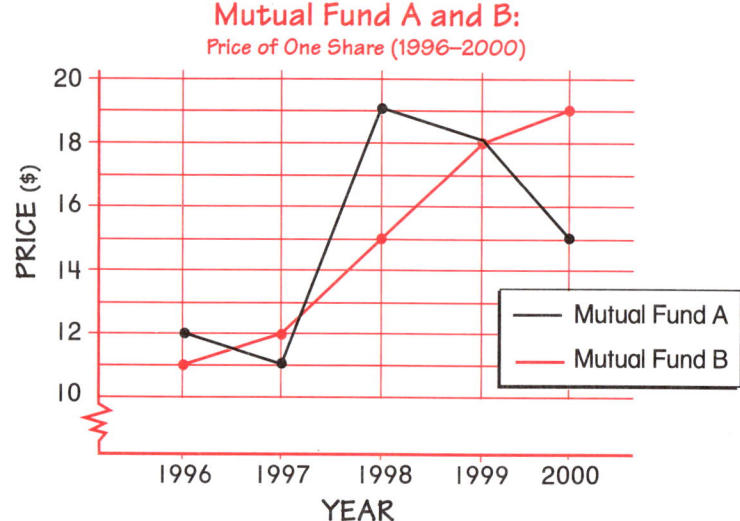

1. At the end of which year were both funds' prices the same?

   a. Look at the graph. Find the point where the lines meet.

   b. Run your finger from the meeting point to the horizontal axis. Mutual Funds A and B:

   What year does the meeting point correspond to? _____

   So, both funds' prices were the same at the end of _____.

2. Which mutual fund had a steady increase in price?

   a. Find the line that slopes up steadily.

   What is the color of that line? _____

   b. Find the name of the fund shown by the red line.

   The name of the fund is _____.

   So, the fund with a steady price increase was _____.

3. What was the highest price that Mutual Fund A reached?

   a. Look at the key. Find the color of Mutual Fund A. Then find the highest point that the fund reached.

   b. Move your finger to the vertical axis to find the price of Mutual Fund A at that point.

   The value of the highest point is $ _____.

   So, the fund's highest price was $ _____.

Chapter 4 | **L4**

PRACTICE

Use the double-line graph to find the information you need to solve the problems.

The graph shows the money people in the United States spent on take-out food and food eaten at a restaurant.

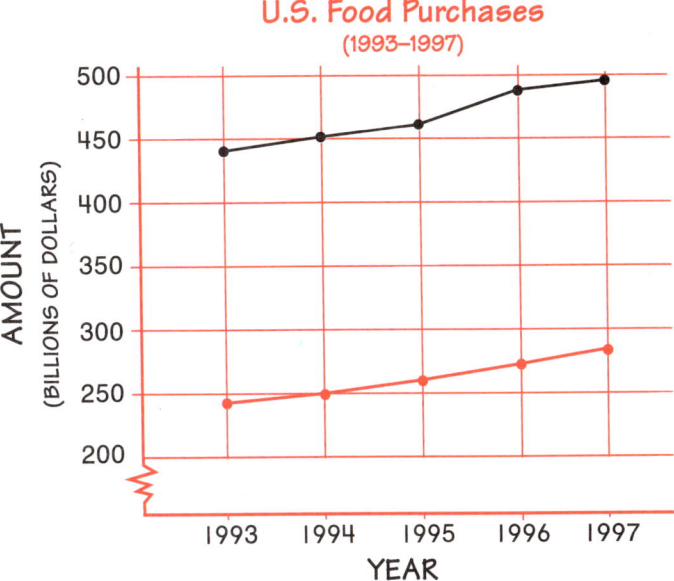

4. Which line shows the amount spent on take-out food?

   _____

5. The vertical axis tells you that the amounts shown are given in _____ of dollars.

6. In which year did people spend the least on eating at restaurants?

   _____

Solve..

7. In 1993, about how much more did people spend on take-out food than they spent at restaurants?

   _____

8. Was there a year between 1993 and 1997 in which people spent more at restaurants than on take-out food? How do you know?

   _____

   _____

9. What trend do both lines show? Explain.

   _____

   _____

• Subtracting Whole Numbers

TEST-TAKING PRACTICE

Choose the best answer for each problem. In the answer section at the bottom of the page, fill in the box of your choice.

Use the graph below for Problems 1–5.

The double-line graph shows the speeds of two girls at different times during a 1-mile walk/run.

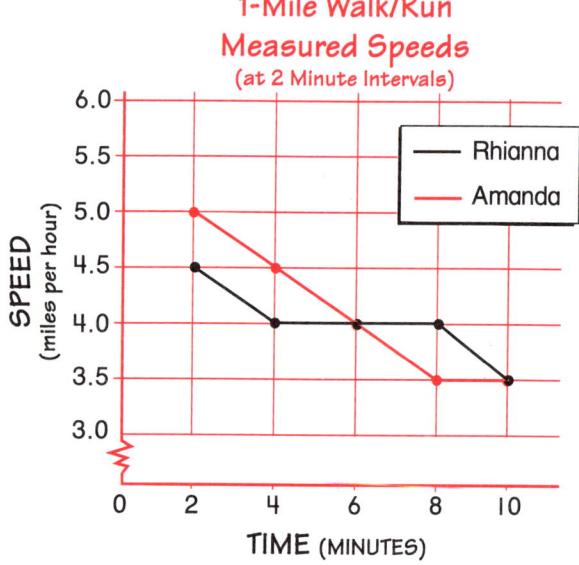

1. How many miles per hour was Amanda going 2 minutes after she started?
   - A 4.0 mph
   - B 4.5 mph
   - C 4.8 mph
   - D 5.0 mph

2. Which choice correctly describes Rhianna's speed from 4 to 8 minutes?
   - J an increase: 4.0 mph to 4.5 mph
   - K a decrease: 4.5 mph to 4.0 mph
   - L a decrease: 4.0 mph to 3.5 mph
   - M 4.0 mph with no change

3. Which choice correctly describes the change in both girls' speeds from 2 to 10 minutes?
   - A increased
   - B decreased
   - C no change
   - D Not given

4. At which two times were the two girls moving at the same speed?
   - J 4 minutes, 8 minutes
   - K 6 minutes, 8 minutes
   - L 6 minutes, 10 minutes
   - M Not given

Write About It

5. How could a track coach use a graph to compare the times of two runners over a track season?

_____
_____
_____
_____
_____
_____
_____
_____
_____

1. A☐ B☐ C☐ D☐
2. J☐ K☐ L☐ M☐
3. A☐ B☐ C☐ D☐
4. J☐ K☐ L☐ M☐

• Subtracting Whole Numbers

Chapters 1–4

Test-Taking Skill: Eliminating Choices

Sometimes you can reach the correct answer to a multiple-choice problem by eliminating choices that are obviously incorrect.

Example 1

Rosemary earned $31.50 for 6 hours of work. How much did she earn per hour?

    A $5.25   **C** $37.50
    B $10.30   **D** 5 hours

Read the question again.

Step 1: Think about what kind of answer you need. The answer to "How much did she earn per hour?" is an amount of money. So, choice **D** must be wrong.

Step 2: Estimate to eliminate choices.

    THINK: Rosemary earned about $30 for 6 hours of work.

    $30 ÷ 6 = $5

    Choice **B**, $10.30, is too large.

    Choice **C**, $37.50, is also too large.

    So, **A** must be the right answer.

Example 2

Each of the buses used for a field trip seats 40 passengers. There are 278 students going on the trip. How many buses will be needed?

    J 6.95   **L** 10
    K 7   **M** 40

Step 1: Think about what kind of answer you need. The number of buses must be a whole number, so choice _____ must be wrong.

Step 2: Find an easy number—choice **L**—and use mental math. If this answer is correct, then the buses will hold 10 × 40, or 400 passengers. The answer is too large, so choice **L** must be wrong, and so must choice _____.

Step 3: Solve by elimination. The correct answer must be choice _____.

• Test-Taking Skill

TEST-TAKING PRACTICE

Choose the best answer for each problem. In the answer section at the bottom of this page, fill in the box of your choice.

Use the bar graph to solve problems 1–3.

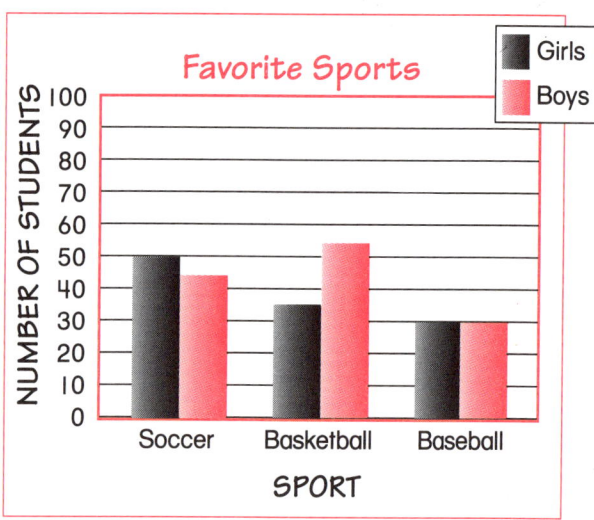

1. How many students chose soccer as their favorite sport?
   A 45
   B 50
   C 95
   D 180

2. How many more boys than girls chose basketball as their favorite sport?
   J 20
   K 35
   L 55
   M 90

3. How many more boys chose basketball as their favorite sport than chose baseball?
   A 5
   B 25
   C 30
   D 55

4. Roberto earned $117 for 18 hours of work. How much did he earn per hour?
   J 6 hours
   K $6.50
   L $10
   M $18

5. Mrs. Ridgeway is sewing shirts for the class play. Each shirt uses $1\frac{1}{3}$ yd of material. She has 10 yards of material. How many shirts can she make?
   A 2
   B 6
   C 7
   D 10

6. At a pizza party each person ate 2 slices of pizza. Each pizza has 8 slices. If they ate a total of 12 pizzas, how many people were there?
   J 12
   K 48
   L 96
   M Not given

7. An inkjet printer can print $4\frac{1}{2}$ pages per minute. At that rate, how many minutes will it take to print 20 pages?
   A 4 pages
   B 4 minutes
   C $4\frac{4}{9}$ pages
   D $4\frac{4}{9}$ minutes

Writing an Equation

You can solve many math problems by writing an equation. When you write an equation, you represent the problem with symbols and numbers. This can help you plan how to solve a problem.

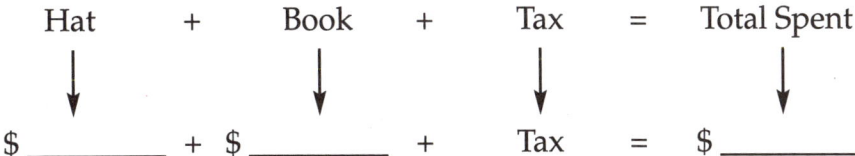

Example

Tina bought a hat for $12.50 and a book for $8.95. With tax, she spent a total of $22.52. How much tax did Tina pay?

A. First, write the problem as a word equation.

    Hat   +   Book   +   Tax   =   Total Spent

B. Fill in the numbers you know in the word equation.

    Hat   +   Book   +   Tax   =   Total Spent

    $ _____ + $ _____ + Tax = $ _____

C. Choose a variable to stand for the number you don't know.

You might choose t for tax.

    12.50   +   8.95   +   Tax   =   22.52

    12.50   +   8.95   + t =   22.52

> When you write an equation, leave out dollar signs, units, and abbreviations. They can be confused with a variable.

D. Solve for t.

    12.50   +   8.95   + t =   22.52

Simplify: _____   + t =   22.52

Write as a related equation: t = 22.52 − 21.45

    t = _____

E. Check your answer by substituting it back into the original equation.

$12.50 + $8.95 + $1.07 = $22.52

The tax that Tina paid was $ _____ .

• Variables and Expressions

GUIDED PRACTICE

1. Art spent a total of $47.93 on two shirts and a cap. Each shirt cost $18.99. How much did the cap cost?

   a. Write a word equation that shows the problem's information.

   Shirt + Shirt + Cap = Total spent

   b. Fill in the numbers you know in the word equation. Use a variable for the number you don't know. Then simplify.

   _____ + _____ + _____ = 47.93

   _____ + _____ = 47.93

   Rewrite as a related subtraction equation. Then solve.

   47.93 − _____ = _____

   c. Check your answer. Substitute your answer into the original equation.

   _____ + _____ + _____ = _____

   The cap cost $ _____ .

2. Sylvia used 32.5 meters of fence to enclose this yard. How wide is the yard at its widest point?

   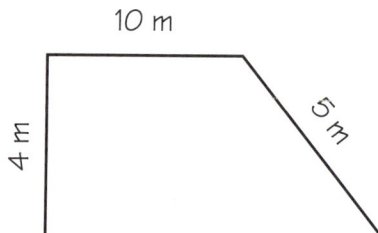

   a. Write a word equation that shows the problem's information.

   Sum of all 4 sides = Total fence used

   b. Fill in the numbers you know in the equation. Use a variable for the number you don't know. Then simplify.

   _____ + _____ + _____ + _____ = 32.5

   _____ + _____ = 32.5

   Rewrite as a related subtraction equation. Then solve.

   32.5 − _____ = _____

   c. Check your answer. Substitute your answer into the original equation.

   _____ + _____ + _____ + _____ = _____

   The yard is _____ m wide at its widest point.

PRACTICE

For problems 3 and 4, write a word equation showing each problem's information. Then write the numbers you know and a variable in the equation, and solve.

3. Patricia ran 23.2 mi last week on three different days. She ran 4.3 mi on Wednesday and 10.5 mi on Friday. **How far did she run on Monday?**

4. Kiko spent $80.54 to buy two lamps. Before tax, one lamp cost $35.99, and the other cost $39.99. **How much tax did Kiko pay?**

Solve

Use the map at right to solve problem 5.

5. Kel drove from Eastlake to Enders, then to Baylor, and then on to Eastlake. His total distance was 63 miles. **How far is it from Enders to Baylor?**

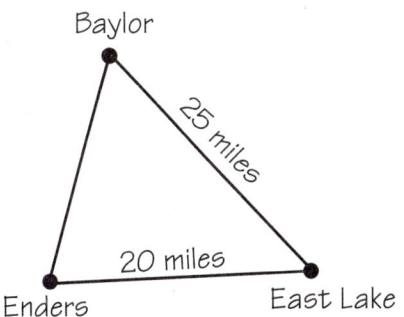

6. To make 64 oz of punch, Haley used 32 oz of orange juice, 8 oz of cranberry punch, and some lemonade. **How much lemonade was in the punch?**

7. Yaron spent $75.50 on two concert tickets, including the fee charged by the ticket agent. Each ticket cost $35. **What fee did he pay to the ticket agent?**

• Variables and Expressions

TEST-TAKING PRACTICE

Choose the best answer for each problem. In the answer section at the bottom of this page, fill in the box of your choice.

1. On a 1,700-mi trip from Houston to San Francisco, Mike drove 720 mi the first day and 610 mi on the second day. How many miles did he drive on the last day?

   Which of the following equations could be used to solve this problem?
   A $720 + n + 1,700 = 610$
   B $720 + 610 + n = 1,700$
   C $720 - 610 + n = 1,700$
   D $1,700 + 720 + 610 = n$

2. Gwen put the bookcase and table shown below alongside an 18-ft wall. How much space is left on the wall for other furniture?

bookcase	table
8 ft	3 ft

   J 7 ft
   K 10 ft
   L 11 ft
   M 18 ft

3. Tim bought a book for $18.25 and a tote bag. He received $6.50 in change from a $50 bill. How much did the tote bag cost?
   A $24.75
   B $25.00
   C $25.25
   D $50.00

4. At the mall, Nicole bought a lunch that cost $5.99, and her brother bought a lunch that cost $5.95. With tax, the total cost was $12.38. **What tax did they pay?**
   J $0.44
   K $5.99
   L $6.39
   M Not given

Write About It
Write a word equation for the information in the problem. Then write the numbers you know and a variable in the equation, and solve.

5. Gary grew 8 inches over a period of 3 years. In 1998, he grew 3 inches, and in 2000, he grew 2 inches. How many inches did Gary grow in 1999?

---

1. A ☐ B ☐ C ☐ D ☐
2. J ☐ K ☐ L ☐ M ☐
3. A ☐ B ☐ C ☐ D ☐
4. J ☐ K ☐ L ☐ M ☐

Chapter 5 | **L2**

Drawing a Number Line

You can use a number line to help you solve problems that use positive and negative integers.

Example 1

A group of students in Montana recorded the outside temperature at noon and at three o'clock. At noon, the temperature was ⁻3°F. By three o'clock, the temperature had risen 5 degrees. What was the temperature at three o'clock?

THINK: ⁻3 + 5 = ?

A. **Decide how to solve the problem.**

I should count up _____ degrees from ⁻3°F.

B. **Draw a number line.**

Mark the line with a dot to show ⁻3°F.

C. **Use the number line to solve the problem.**

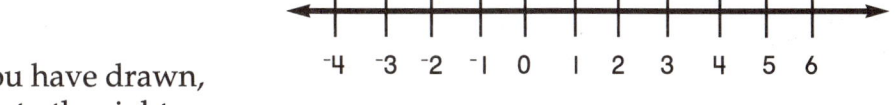

Begin at the dot you have drawn, then move 5 places to the right.

At which number do you end up? _____

So, the temperature at three o'clock was _____ °F.

Example 2

The next day, the high temperature was ⁻4°F. By evening, the temperature had dropped 7°F. What was the temperature that evening?

THINK: ⁻4 + ⁻7 = ?

Step 1: **Decide how to solve the problem.**

I should count down _____ degrees from ⁻4°F.

Step 2: **Use a number line to solve the problem.**

Mark the line with a dot to show ⁻4°F, then move 7 places to the left.

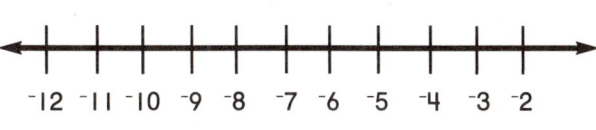

At which number do you end up? _____

The temperature that evening was _____ °F.

• Adding and Subtracting Integers

GUIDED PRACTICE

1. At the start of her experiment, Jeri recorded the temperature of a liquid mixture as ⁻1°C. She then heated the liquid to a temperature of 9°C. By how many degrees did the temperature change? Did it increase or decrease?

    Step 1: **Decide how to solve the problem.**

    I should find the change from _____°C to _____°C.

    Step 2: **Draw a number line.**

    Mark the line with dots to show ⁻1° and 9°C.

    Step 3: **Use the number line to solve the problem.**

    Count the spaces from ⁻1 to 9.

    There are _____ spaces. You need to count up (to the right).

    The temperature changed by _____ degrees.

    Did it increase or decrease? _____

2. At three o'clock, the temperature was 4°F. By midnight, the temperature had dropped to ⁻8°F. How many degrees had the temperature dropped?

    Step 1: **Decide how to solve the problem.**

    I should find the change from _____°F to _____°F.

    Step 2: **Draw a number line.**

    Mark the line with dots to show 4° and ⁻8°F.

    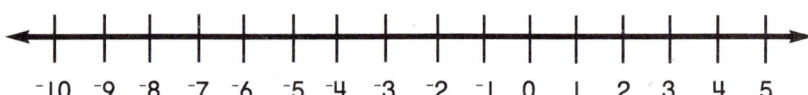

    Step 3: **Use the number line to solve the problem.**

    Count the spaces from 4°F to ⁻8°F: _____

    So, the temperature dropped _____ degrees.

PRACTICE
Mark the number lines to solve each problem.

3. How many degrees warmer is a temperature of ⁻5°C than a temperature of ⁻12°C?

4. At noon, the temperature was 2°F. By evening it was ⁻6°F. How many degrees did the temperature drop?

5. When Neil woke up on Saturday, the temperature was ⁻6°F. By noon, the temperature had risen 5 degrees. What was the temperature at noon?

6. When Janice came home from school, the temperature was ⁻3°F. By evening, the temperature had dropped 9 degrees. What was the temperature that evening?

7. A saltwater solution measures 8°C. The temperature is lowered to ⁻3°C. By how many degrees did the temperature of the solution change? Did it increase or decrease?

• Adding and Subtracting Integers

TEST-TAKING PRACTICE

Choose the best answer for problems 1—5. In the answer section at the bottom of this page, fill in the box of your choice.

1. Which problem is shown on this number line?

   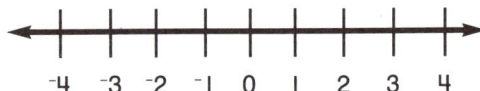

   A $^-2 + 3 = n$ C $5 + {}^-3 = n$
   B $^-3 + 3 = n$ D $3 + {}^-5 = n$

2. Which problem is shown on this number line?

   J $^-4 + 6 = n$ L $2 - 4 = n$
   K $6 - 4 = n$ M $^-6 - 4 = n$

3. The temperature at 9 a.m. was $^-4°F$. During the day, the temperature rose 7 degrees. What was the temperature at the end of the day?
   A $^-11°F$ C $3°F$
   B $-4°F$ D $7°F$

4. The temperature of a liquid mixture measures $-2°C$. The mixture's temperature is lowered 8 degrees. What is its final temperature?
   J $^-10°C$ L $2°C$
   K $^-8°C$ M $6°C$

5. A solution measures $^-3°C$. The solution is heated to $4°C$. By how many degrees did the temperature of the solution change?
   A 4 degrees
   B 7 degrees
   C 8 degrees
   D Not given

Write About It
Write a plan for solving the following problem. Then solve.

6. The temperature inside a garage measures $10°F$. The temperature outside measures $^-8°F$. What is the difference between the two temperatures?

   _____
   _____
   _____
   _____
   _____
   _____
   _____
   _____
   _____

1. A☐ B☐ C☐ D☐   4. J☐ K☐ L☐ M☐
2. J☐ K☐ L☐ M☐   5. A☐ B☐ C☐ D☐
3. A☐ B☐ C☐ D☐

● Adding and Subtracting Integers

Drawing a Picture

You can draw a picture to represent problems that involve position or movement.

Example 1

The top of a mountain is 1,200 ft above sea level. A nearby valley dips 300 ft below sea level. How far above the valley floor is the mountain top?

Step 1: **Draw a picture to show the mountain and the valley.**

Use a line to show sea level. Show the mountain top at 1200 ft above sea level and the valley floor at 300 ft below sea level.

Step 2: **Use the picture to solve the problem.**

Add the distances from sea level.

1200 ft + 300 ft = _____ ft

So, the mountain top is _____ ft above the valley floor.

Example 2

An airplane flew 350 miles to the east and then 500 miles to the west. How far is the airplane from its starting point, and in what direction?

Step 1: Draw a line. Show east and west. Mark the line with a dot to show the starting point. Let the starting point be 0.

Step 2: Draw an arrow to show the airplane's 350-mile trip to the east. Draw an arrow to show the airplane's 500-mile trip to the west. Mark numbers on the line to help you.

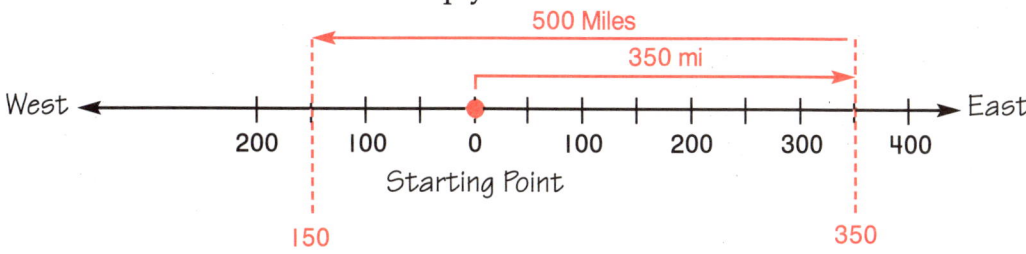

Step 3: Solve. What number on the line does the last arrow point to?

_____ miles west

So, the airplane is _____ of its starting point.

• Adding and Subtracting Integers

GUIDED PRACTICE

1. The top of an oil rig is 250 ft above sea level. A diving vessel is 1,200 ft beneath sea level. What is the distance from the diving vessel to the top of the oil rig?

   The picture to the right shows the position of the oil rig and the diving vessel.

   Step 1: Label sea level. Label the oil rig and the diving vessel.

   Step 2: Show the feet above and below sea level.

   Step 3: Use the picture to solve the problem. Add.

   _____ ft + _____ ft = _____ ft

   So, the distance from the diving vessel to the top of the oil rig is _____ ft.

2. Scott drives 325 miles west to visit a friend and then 200 miles back to the east to see his parents. How far is Scott from his starting point, and in what direction?

   Step 1: Show east and west on the line below. Mark the line with a dot to show Scott's starting point. Let the starting point be 0.

   Step 2: Mark numbers on the line.

   Step 3: Show Scott's trip 325 miles to the west. Draw an arrow to the left.

   Step 4: Show Scott's trip 200 miles to the east. Draw an arrow to the right.

   West ← — — — — — — — — — — — — — — — — — — → East
   0
   Starting Point

   Step 5: Use the picture to solve the problem. What number on the line does the last arrow point to?

   _____

   Scott is _____ of his starting point.

Chapter 5 L3

PRACTICE

Draw a picture to solve the problem.

3. The bottom of a valley is 400 ft below sea level. An eagle takes off from the valley floor and rises 650 ft. **How far above sea level is the eagle now?**

   Draw a picture.

   _____

4. The top of a mountain is 1,400 ft above sea level. A hiker starts at the top of the mountain. She walks down the mountain into a nearby valley, finishing her walk at 200 ft below sea level. **How many feet did the hiker descend from the top of the mountain to the valley floor?**

   Draw a picture.

   _____

5. A jet flies 800 miles north to one city. After landing, the jet then flies 250 miles south to another city. **How far is the jet from its starting point, and in what direction?**

   Draw a picture.

   _____

• Adding and Subtracting Integers

TEST-TAKING PRACTICE

Choose the best answer for each problem. In the answer section at the bottom of this page, fill in the box of your choice.

1. Jasmine drove east 300 miles to a job interview. Then she drove 500 miles west to another interview. How far is she from her starting point?

   Which of the following pictures could be used to solve this problem?

   A

   B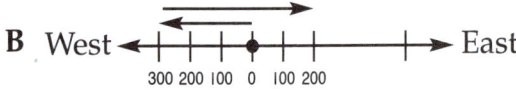

   C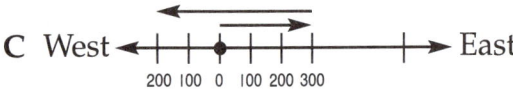

   D Not given

2. A scientist on the deck of a boat is 10 ft above sea level. She drops a rope over the side of the boat. When the rope touches the ocean bottom, it measures 85 ft long. How far below sea level is the ocean bottom?

   J 10 ft
   K 75 ft
   L 85 ft
   M 95 ft

3. A train starts in Aberdeen and travels 900 miles north. Then it travels 1,300 miles south to Virginia Beach. How far is the train from Aberdeen?

   A 400 miles south
   B 400 miles north
   C 900 miles north
   D 1,300 miles south

Write About It

Write a plan for solving the following problem. Then solve.

4. Linda drove 30 miles east, 20 miles west, and then 60 miles east. How far is she from her starting point, and in what direction?

   _____
   _____
   _____
   _____
   _____
   _____
   _____
   _____
   _____
   _____

1. A ☐ B ☐ C ☐ D ☐
2. J ☐ K ☐ L ☐ M ☐
3. A ☐ B ☐ C ☐ D ☐

• Adding and Subtracting Integers

Chapter 6 | **L1**

Drawing a Number Line

You can show information on a number line to help you add and subtract mixed numbers.

Example

Kel works at the school refreshment stand. He needs to make 10 gallons of lemonade. If he mixes $7\frac{7}{8}$ gallons of water with $1\frac{1}{6}$ gallons of sweetened lemon juice, will he have enough lemonade?

A. Decide what you need to find out.

Is the sum of $7\frac{7}{8}$ and $1\frac{1}{6}$ less than _____?

B. Use benchmarks to approximate each number.

- If the numerator is close to zero compared to the denominator, the fraction is close to zero—for example: $\frac{1}{6}, \frac{3}{15}, \frac{8}{50}$

- If the numerator is about half the denominator, the fraction is close to $\frac{1}{2}$ — for example: $\frac{3}{7}, \frac{8}{15}, \frac{21}{20}$

- If the numerator and denominator are about the same, the fraction is close to 1—for example: $\frac{5}{6}, \frac{14}{15}, \frac{47}{50}$

$\frac{7}{8}$ is close to 1. So, $7\frac{7}{8}$ is close to _____.

$\frac{1}{6}$ is close to 0. So, $1\frac{1}{6}$ is close to _____.

C. Use a number line. Mark the line with a dot a little to the left of 8. Then count on from the dot a little more than 1 space to the right.

Is the new position on the line greater or less than 10? _____

So, Kel's recipe _____ make enough lemonade.

• Adding and Subtracting Mixed Numbers

GUIDED PRACTICE

1. An electrician cuts a $6\frac{5}{8}$-foot length from an $10\frac{5}{12}$-foot roll of wire. Can she cut a 3-foot length from the remaining wire?

   Step 1: Decide what you need to find out.

   Is the difference between $10\frac{5}{12}$ and $6\frac{5}{8}$ greater than _____?

   Step 2: Use benchmarks to approximate each number.

   $\frac{5}{12}$ is close to _____, so $10\frac{5}{12}$ is close to _____.

   $\frac{5}{8}$ is close to _____, so $6\frac{5}{8}$ is close to _____.

   Step 3: Use a number line.

   Mark the line with a dot at $10\frac{1}{2}$.

   Move about $6\frac{1}{2}$ spaces to the left.

   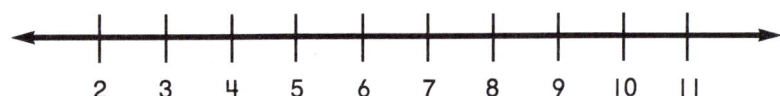

   Is the new position on the line greater or less than 3? _____

   So, the electrician _____ cut a 3 ft length from the remaining wire.

2. Nelson needs $1\frac{1}{3}$ c of wheat flour and $1\frac{3}{4}$ c of corn flour for a corn bread recipe. How many cups of flour does the recipe call for?

   Step 1: Decide what you need to find out.

   What is the sum of _____ and _____?

   Step 2: Decide if you can use approximate numbers.

   You need an exact sum, so the answer is _____.

   Step 3: Use the LCD to write the numbers as equivalent fractions, and add.

   $\frac{1}{3} = \frac{4}{12}$ $\frac{3}{4} = \frac{9}{12}$

   $1\frac{4}{12} + 1\frac{9}{12} = $ _____

   Step 4: Check your answer on a number line.

   Mark a dot to show $1\frac{1}{3}$. Move right a little less than 2 spaces.

   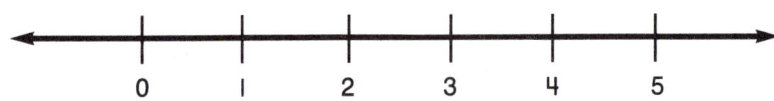

   So, the recipe calls for _____ cups of flour.

PRACTICE

Solve. Use benchmark fractions to help you.

Mark on the number line to solve each problem.

3. Janell cuts a $2\frac{1}{2}$-ft shelf from a board that is 8 ft long. She needs another piece $4\frac{7}{8}$ ft long. Does she have enough wood left for the piece?

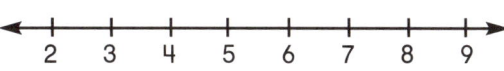

_____

4. Perry has $2\frac{1}{2}$ pt of orange juice and $3\frac{2}{3}$ pt of grapefruit juice. Can he pour them both into a container that holds 5 pt without it overflowing?

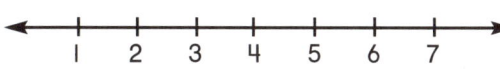

_____

5. Julia has 8 balls of yarn. She uses $5\frac{1}{8}$ balls to knit a sweater. She needs $1\frac{5}{6}$ balls to make a scarf. Does she have enough yarn left?

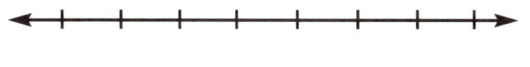

_____

Find the LCD to solve. Use a number line to check your answer.

6. Jeff rides his bike $5\frac{3}{10}$ miles to Streetsville, and then rides another $2\frac{2}{5}$ miles to Logan's house. How many miles does he ride?

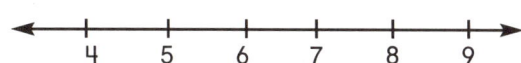

_____

7. Christian is mailing a package of 2 books. The package weighs $2\frac{1}{4}$ lb with 1 book, and $4\frac{5}{8}$ lb with 2 books. How much does the second book weigh?

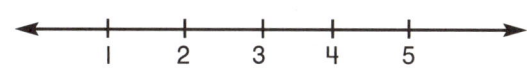

_____

8. Gladys's puppy weighed $3\frac{1}{3}$ lb when she brought it home. Now it weighs 8 lb. How much weight has the puppy gained?

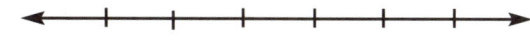

_____

• Adding and Subtracting Mixed Numbers

TEST-TAKING PRACTICE

Choose the best answer for each problem. In the answer section at the bottom of this page, fill in the box of your choice.

1. Catalina poured $2\frac{2}{3}$ qt of milk from a full 4-qt jug. Which of the following statements about the jug is true?
   A   It has less than 1 qt of milk.
   B   It has about 1 qt of milk.
   C   It has about 2 qt of milk.
   D   It has about 3 qt of milk.

2. A child was $18\frac{7}{8}$ inches at birth. Since then, he has doubled his length. Which of the following statements is true about the child now?
   J   He is about 18 in. tall.
   K   He is about 30 in. tall.
   L   He is exactly 36 in. tall.
   M   He is more than 36 in. tall.

3. Vernon cut $3\frac{5}{6}$ inches from a 12-inch strip of wood. How much wood is left?
   A $3\frac{5}{6}$ in.   C $8\frac{1}{6}$ in.
   B   8 in.   D $9\frac{1}{6}$ in.

4. Reynaldo ran $3\frac{1}{8}$ miles yesterday and $2\frac{3}{4}$ miles today. About how many miles did he run in all?
   J   about 4 mi   L   about 6 mi
   K   about $5\frac{1}{2}$ mi   M   about $6\frac{1}{2}$ mi

5. Fran pours $6\frac{7}{8}$ gallons of gas into a tank that already contains $1\frac{1}{4}$ gallons. About how much gas is in the tank?
   A   about 7 gal
   B   about $7\frac{1}{2}$ gal
   C   about 8 gal
   D   about $8\frac{1}{2}$ gal

Write About It
Write a plan for solving the following problem. Then solve.

6. The cafeteria workers want to put two tables along a wall that is 16 feet long. One table is $7\frac{7}{8}$ ft long. The other is $8\frac{5}{6}$ ft long. Will both tables fit?

   _____
   _____
   _____
   _____
   _____
   _____

1. A ☐ B ☐ C ☐ D ☐   4. J ☐ K ☐ L ☐ M ☐
2. J ☐ K ☐ L ☐ M ☐   5. A ☐ B ☐ C ☐ D ☐
3. A ☐ B ☐ C ☐ D ☐

Underlining Needed Information

Some problems ask you to find information on a product label. You may find it helpful to underline or circle the information that you need to solve the problem.

Example

The labels below show the nutritional information of two drinks. How much more sodium is there in 30 fluid ounces of *J for Juice* than there is in 30 fluid ounces of *Fancy Fruit*?

Fancy Fruit			J for Juice		
Nutritional Facts			Nutritional Facts		
Serv. Size 12 fl oz			Serv. Size 12 fl oz		
Amount per Serving			**Amount per Serving**		
Calories	140		Calories	140	
		% Daily Value*			% Daily Value*
Total Fat	0 g	0%	Total Fat	0 g	0%
Sodium	50 mg	2%	Sodium	70 mg	3%
Total Carb	39 g	13%	Total Carb	38 g	13%
Sugars	39 g		Sugars	38 g	
Protein	0 g		Protein	0 g	
*Percent Daily Values are based on a 2,000 calorie diet.			*Percent Daily Values are based on a 2,000 calorie diet.		

A. Find the serving size on each label and underline or circle it.

How many servings is 30 fluid ounces?

30 ÷ _____ = _____ servings

B. Find and underline or circle the sodium content per serving of each drink.

Multiply to find the sodium in $2\frac{1}{2}$ servings.

Fancy Fruit: _____ mg × $2\frac{1}{2}$ = 125 mg

J for Juice: _____ mg × $2\frac{1}{2}$ = 175 mg

C. Subtract to find the difference in the amount of sodium.

_____ mg − _____ mg = _____ mg

So, there are _____ mg more sodium in 30 fl oz of *J for Juice*.

• Multiplying and Dividing Fractions

GUIDED PRACTICE

Use the nutrition labels to solve the problems.

Tomato Sauce	Pasta
Nutritional Facts	Nutritional Facts
Serving Size $\frac{1}{2}$ cup	Serving Size 2 oz
Servings per Container about 8	Servings per Container about 8
Amount per Serving	**Amount per Serving**
Calories 140	Calories 210
Calories from Fat 40	Calories from Fat 10
% Daily Value*	% Daily Value*
Total Fat 4.5 g 7%	**Total Fat** 1 g 2%
Saturated Fat 1.5 g 8%	Saturated Fat 0 g 0%
Sodium 610 mg 25%	**Sodium** 0 mg 0%
Total Carbohydrate 23 g 8%	**Total Carbohydrate** 42 g 14%
Dietary Fiber 2 g 8%	Dietary Fiber 2 g 8%
Sugars 16 g	Sugars 2 g
Protein 2 g	**Protein** 7 g
*Percent Daily Values are based on a 2,000 calorie diet.	*Percent Daily Values are based on a 2,000 calorie diet.

1. How much protein is there in the whole box of pasta?

   On the pasta label, underline or circle the servings per container and the protein per serving.

   Multiply to find the protein per container.

   Servings per container x Protein per serving = Protein per container

   _____ x _____ g = _____ g

   So, the box contains _____ grams of protein.

2. How many grams of carbohydrates are there in 2 cups of tomato sauce?

   Step 1: On the sauce label, underline or circle the serving size.

   Divide to find number of servings in 2 cups.

   2 ÷ _____ = _____ servings

   Step 2: On the sauce label, underline the amount of carbohydrates per serving.

   Multiply to find the carbohydrates in 4 servings.

   _____ g x 4 = _____ g

   So, 2 cups of tomato sauce contain _____ grams of carbohydrates.

PRACTICE

Use the nutrition labels to solve the problems.

Cereal	Powdered Cocoa Mix
Nutritional Facts	Nutritional Facts
Serving Size $\frac{3}{4}$ cup	Serving Size $\frac{1}{3}$ cup (46g)
Servings per Container about 13	Servings per Container about 13
Amount per Serving	**Amount per Serving**
Calories 120	Calories 190
Calories from Fat 10	Calories from Fat 25
% Daily Value*	% Daily Value*
Total Fat 1 g 2%	Total Fat 4 g 6%
Saturated Fat 0 g 0%	Saturated Fat 1.5 g 8%
Sodium 140 mg 6%	Sodium 210 mg 9%
Total Carbohydrate 28 g 9%	Total Carbohydrate 37 g 12%
Dietary Fiber 2 g 8%	Dietary Fiber 1 g 4%
Sugars 10 g	Sugars 29 g
Protein 3 g	Protein 2 g
*Percent Daily Values are based on a 2,000 calorie diet. Your daily values may be higher or lower depending on your calorie needs.	*Percent Daily Values are based on a 2,000 calorie diet. Your daily values may be higher or lower depending on your calorie needs.

3. How many grams of carbohydrates are in $1\frac{1}{2}$ cups of cereal?

4. About how many cups of cereal are in a container?

5. How many grams of protein are in 1 cup of cocoa powder?

6. About how many grams of cocoa are in the container?

7. How many servings of cereal would you have to eat to take in 600 calories?

8. How many more calories are there in a cup of cocoa powder than in a cup of cereal?

9. How many cups of cocoa powder contain 10 grams of protein?

10. How many grams of sugars are there in 6 cups of cereal?

• Multiplying and Dividing Fractions

TEST-TAKING PRACTICE

Use the nutrition label from a box of raisins to choose the best answer for each problem. In the answer section at the bottom of this page, fill in the box of your choice.

Raisins
Nutritional Facts
Serving Size $\frac{1}{4}$ cup (40g)
Servings per Container about 11
Amount per Serving
Calories   130

		% Daily Value*
Total Fat	0 g	0%
Saturated Fat	0 g	0%
Sodium	10 mg	0%
Total Carbohydrate	31 g	10%
Dietary Fiber	2 g	9%
Sugars	29 g	
Protein	1 g	

*Percent Daily Values are based on a 2,000 calorie diet.

1. How many calories are there in 2 cups of raisins?
   - A 130 cal
   - B 520 cal
   - C 260 cal
   - D 1,040 cal

2. How many milligrams of sodium are in $1\frac{1}{2}$ servings of raisins?
   - J 10 mg
   - K 15 mg
   - L 20 mg
   - M 30 mg

3. About how many grams of raisins are there in a box?
   - A 440 g
   - B 160 g
   - C 40 g
   - D 11 g

4. How many grams of carbohydrates does a whole box of raisins contain?
   - J less than 300 g
   - K more than 300 g
   - L exactly 300 g
   - M cannot tell from the data

5. How many grams of protein are there in a cup of raisins?
   - A 11 g
   - B 4 g
   - C 1 g
   - D Not given

Write About It
Write a plan for solving the following problem. Then solve.

6. A recipe calls for 3 cups of raisins. Will one box of raisins be enough?

_____
_____
_____
_____
_____
_____
_____
_____
_____

1. A☐ B☐ C☐ D☐
2. J☐ K☐ L☐ M☐
3. A☐ B☐ C☐ D☐
4. J☐ K☐ L☐ M☐
5. A☐ B☐ C☐ D☐

• Multiplying and Dividing Fractions

Chapter 6 | **L3**

Solving Multi-Step Problems

A problem may take more than two steps to solve. It can be helpful to decide what questions you need to ask in order to solve the problem.

EXAMPLE

Deanna is making bookcases. Each shelf must be $3\frac{1}{2}$ feet long. She cuts the shelves from boards that are each 14 feet long and cost $18. If Deanna spends a total of $108 on boards, how many $3\frac{1}{2}$-foot shelves can she make?

Step 1: List the questions you will need to answer.

    a. How many shelves can she cut from each board?

    b. How many boards did she buy?

    c. How many shelves can she make from all the boards?

Step 2: Write a word equation for each question.

    a. How many shelves can she cut from each board?

    Length of board ÷ Length of shelf = Number of shelves per board

    b. How many boards did she buy?

    Amount Deanna spent ÷ Cost per board = Number of boards

    c. How many shelves can she make from all the boards?

    Number of boards x Number of shelves per board = Number of shelves

Step 3: Substitute amounts in the word equations to solve.

    a. Length of board ÷ Length of shelf = Number of shelves per board

        14 ft ÷ $3\frac{1}{2}$ ft = _____

    b. Amount Deanna spent ÷ Cost per board = Number of boards

        $108 ÷ $18 = _____

    c. Number of boards x Number of shelves per board = Number of shelves

        _____ x _____ = _____

So, Deanna can make _____ shelves.

• Dividing with Fractions

GUIDED PRACTICE

1. A museum raises $12,000 at a special event. Tickets cost $75 per person. At the event, the museum serves $1\frac{5}{8}$ pounds of fish to each table. If each table seats 4 people, how many pounds of fish does the museum need?

   a. For each question you need to answer, write a word equation.

How many people are at the event?
Money raised ÷ _____ = Number of people
How many tables are used?
Number of people ÷ _____ = Number of tables
How many pounds of fish are needed?
_____ x Pounds of fish per table = Pounds of fish

   b. Substitute amounts in the word equations to solve.

   Money raised ÷ Ticket price = Number of people
   _____   ÷   _____   =   _____

   Number of people ÷ People per table = Number of tables
   _____   ÷   _____   =   _____

   Number of tables x Pounds of fish per table = Pounds of fish
   _____   x   _____   =   _____

   So, the museum needs _____ pounds of fish.

Chapter 6 L3

PRACTICE

Write questions and use word equations to help you solve.

2. A sculptor estimates that each sculpture in a series will take $12\frac{1}{2}$ pounds of cement. Cement comes in 50-pound bags. The sculptures will be placed in 5 groups of 4 sculptures each. How many bags of cement should he buy?

Question	Word Equation

Solve.

_____

_____

3. Brooke jogged $2\frac{1}{4}$ miles each day for 4 days. Then she jogged $2\frac{1}{2}$ miles each day for the next three days. How many miles did she jog during the week?

Question	Word Equation

Solve.

_____

_____

• Dividing with Fractions

TEST-TAKING PRACTICE

Choose the best answer for each problem. In the answer section at the bottom of the page, fill in the box of your choice.

1. Barnaby is making square picture frames with sides of $5\frac{1}{2}$ inches. He cuts the frames from strips of wood that are 70 inches long. Each strip of wood costs $12. If Barnaby spends a total of $60 on wood, how many picture frames can he make?
   A 5 frames
   B 15 frames
   C 50 frames
   D 80 frames

2. During the first week of vacation, Jim cycles 20 miles each day. The following week he only cycled 6 days, 25 miles a day. How much farther did he cycle in the second week than in the first week?
   J 5 miles
   K 10 miles
   L 45 miles
   M 150 miles

3. As a prize on the "You'll Only Get Part of It" game show, Robin receives $\frac{1}{2}$ of $750, $\frac{1}{3}$ of $525, and $\frac{1}{4}$ of $364. How much does Robin receive in all?
   A $175
   B $375
   C $550
   D $641

4. Mr. Ramos is laying a path with 1-foot-square cement stones, each made with $4\frac{1}{6}$ pounds of cement. Cement comes in 50-pound bags. If the path is 36 feet long, how many bags of cement will Mr. Ramos use?
   J 3 bags   L 6 bags
   K 4 bags   M Not given

Write About It

Write a plan for solving the following problem. Then solve.

5. Simone is making a recipe that uses $3\frac{1}{2}$ cups flour. She estimates that there are 14 cups of flour in a 5-lb bag. A bag of flour costs $3. How much would the flour cost for 12 batches of the recipe?

1. A☐ B☐ C☐ D☐   3. A☐ B☐ C☐ D☐
2. J☐ K☐ L☐ M☐   4. J☐ K☐ L☐ M☐

• Dividing with Fractions

Chapters 1—6

Test-Taking Skill: Writing a Plan

On some tests you need to explain how to solve a problem. Remember to explain your thinking and show your calculations.

Example

At the Quick and Go, 6 members of a club each bought a slice of pizza for $1.50. The other members each bought a burger. If there are 14 members of the club and they spent a total of $27.00, what is the price of a burger at Quick and Go?

A. Read the problem carefully. Decide what is being asked.

The problem asks for the price of one burger—a money amount.

B. Make a plan.

Step 1:   Multiply 6 x $1.50 to find the total pizza cost.

Step 2:   Subtract the total pizza cost from $27.00 to find out the total burger cost.

Step 3:   Subtract 6 from 14 to find the number of burgers bought.

Step 4:   Divide the total burger cost by the number of burgers bought.

C. Solve the problem. Show your calculations. Change your plan if you need to.

Step 1:   6 x $1.50 = $ _____

Step 2: $27.00 – $ _____ = $ _____

Step 3:   14 – 6 = 8

Step 4: $ _____ ÷ 8 = $ _____

D. Remember to give your solution in the correct form.

The price of a burger at Quick and Go is $ _____ .

• Test-Taking Skill

TEST-TAKING PRACTICE

Write a plan to solve the problem. Then solve. Show your work.

1. There are 12 pieces of fruit in a basket. Of these, $\frac{1}{3}$ are oranges, $\frac{1}{4}$ are grapefruit, $\frac{1}{6}$ are bananas, and the rest are strawberries. How many strawberries are in the bowl?

2. What is the value of y?

Input	3	5	10	y
Output	4.5	7.5	15	27

● Test-Taking Skill

Writing a Word Equation

Showing the information in a problem involving speed, time, and distance in a word equation can help you solve the problem.

Example 1

The Packard family drove from New York to Denver in 40 hours. They traveled a distance of 2,100 miles. What was the family's average speed?

A. Write a word equation for average speed, time, and distance.

    Average speed   x   Time   =   Distance

B. Substitute a variable and amounts from the problem.

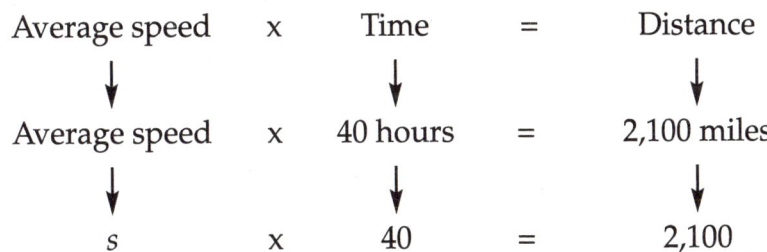

C. Solve the equation, and answer the question.

    $s \times \dfrac{40}{40} = \dfrac{2{,}100}{40}$

So, $s =$ _____

Their average speed was _____ miles/hour.

Example 2

The DeSotos drove for 6.5 hours at an average speed of 48 miles per hour. How far did they travel?

A. Write a word equation for average speed, time, and distance, and substitute a variable and amounts from the problem.

    Average speed   x   Time   =   Distance
    ↓   ↓   ↓
    48 miles/hour   x   6.5 hours   = d
    ↓   ↓   ↓
    48   x   6.5   = d

B. Solve the equation, and answer the question.

    d =   48   x   6.5

So, $d =$ _____

They traveled _____ miles.

• Multiplying and Dividing Decimals

GUIDED PRACTICE

1. A jet plane flies 5,400 miles from Los Angeles, California, to London, England. If the jet travels at an average speed of 500 miles per hour, how long will the trip take?

   Step 1: Write the word equation.

   _____ x _____ = _____

   Step 2: Substitute with numbers and a variable.

   _____ x Time = _____
   ↓   ↓   ↓
   _____ x t = _____

   Step 3: Solve the equation.

   $500 \times t = 5,400$

   $\dfrac{500 \times t}{500} = \dfrac{5,400}{500}$ So, $t =$ _____

   So, the trip will take _____ hours.

2. It took Terry 2.5 hours to ride the 22.5 miles to her uncle's house. What was her average speed for the trip?

   Step 1: Write the word equation.

   Average speed   x   _____   =   _____

   Step 2: Substitute with numbers and a variable.

   Average speed   x   _____   =   _____
   ↓   ↓   ↓
   s x   _____   =   _____

   Step 3: Solve the equation.

   s x _____ = _____

   So, $s =$ _____

   Terry's average speed was _____ miles/hour.

Chapter 7 | **L1**

PRACTICE

Write a word equation, using amounts from the problem. Then solve.

3. In 1932, Amelia Earhart became the first woman to fly a plane across the Atlantic. She flew approximately 2,025 miles, from Canada to Ireland, in about 15 hours. What was Earhart's average speed on the trip?

_____

_____

4. A rocket must reach a speed of about 25,000 miles/hour to break free of Earth's gravity and head out into space. Traveling at that speed, how long would it take a rocket to cover 200,000 miles?

_____

_____

5. The distance from Atlanta, Georgia, to New Orleans, Louisiana, is 517 miles. If Ms. Chenier makes the trip in 10 hours, at what average speed does she drive?

_____

_____

6. The Concorde is a high-speed jet that travels at about 1,200 miles per hour. How long would it take the Concorde to fly from Paris to New York, a distance of 3,624 miles?

_____

_____

● Multiplying and Dividing Decimals

TEST-TAKING PRACTICE

Choose the best answer for each problem. In the answer section at the bottom of the page, fill in the box of your choice.

1. Light travels at a speed of about 186,000 miles per second. Which equation could be used to find how long it takes for light to travel the 240,000 miles from the moon to the earth?
   A 186,000 ÷ 240,000 = t
   B 186,000 x t = 240,000
   C t x 240,000 = 186,000
   D 186,000 x 240,000 = t

2. It took Mr. Marina $34\frac{1}{3}$ hours to drive 1,790 miles from San Antonio to San Francisco. Which equation could be used to find his average speed?
   J $34\frac{1}{3}$ x 1,790 = s
   K $34\frac{1}{3}$ ÷ s = 1,790
   L 1,790 x s = $34\frac{1}{3}$
   M s x $34\frac{1}{3}$ = 1,790

3. Kelly ran $6\frac{1}{3}$ miles in 2 hours. At what average speed did she run?
   A 2 mph
   B $3\frac{1}{6}$ mph
   C $6\frac{1}{3}$ mph
   D $12\frac{2}{3}$ mph

4. Webster drove for 8 hours at an average speed of 46.3 miles/hour. How far did he travel?
   J 5.79 miles
   K 54.3 miles
   L 370.4 miles
   M 2,963.2 miles

5. The first flight to the North Pole took place in 1926. The flight took off in Norway, and covered about 1,550 miles at an average speed of 100 miles/hour. How long did it take to reach the North Pole?
   A 15.5 hours
   B 16.5 hours
   C 155 hours
   D Not given

Write About It
Write a plan for solving the following problem. Then solve.

6. Sierra and her brother want to drive from Los Angeles to Dallas, a distance of 1,425 miles. If they do not exceed 55 miles/hour, what is the least amount of time they will need to make the trip?

_____
_____
_____
_____
_____
_____
_____
_____

1. A ☐ B ☐ C ☐ D ☐
2. J ☐ K ☐ L ☐ M ☐
3. A ☐ B ☐ C ☐ D ☐
4. J ☐ K ☐ L ☐ M ☐
5. A ☐ B ☐ C ☐ D ☐

• Multiplying and Dividing Decimals

Writing Word Proportions

Some rate problems compare two quantities. Showing the information in a word proportion can help you solve rate problems.

Example

In January, Los Angeles has an average of 10 hours of daylight during each 24-hour day. How many hours of daylight does Los Angeles have during each 120-hour period in January?

A. Write a word proportion to show the problem.

Make sure that the rates are equivalent.

$$\text{THINK:} \quad \frac{\text{part}}{\text{whole}} = \frac{\text{part}}{\text{whole}}$$

$$\frac{\text{daylight in 24 hours}}{\text{24 hours}} = \frac{\text{daylight in 120 hours}}{\text{120 hours}}$$

B. Rewrite the word proportion with a variable and amounts from the problem.

$$\frac{\text{10 hours}}{\text{24 hours}} = \frac{\text{daylight in 120 hours}}{\text{120 hours}}$$

$$\frac{10}{24} = \frac{d}{120}$$

C. Solve the proportion.

$$\frac{10}{24} = \frac{d}{120}$$

$$d \times 24 = 10 \times 120$$

$$d = 50$$

So, Los Angeles has _____ hours of daylight in each 120-hour period.

• Solving Proportions

GUIDED PRACTICE

1. There are 210 calories in 2 ounces of uncooked pasta. How many calories are there in 7 ounces of uncooked pasta?

   Step 1: Write a word proportion to show the problem.

   $$\frac{\text{calories in 2 oz}}{2 \text{ oz}} = \frac{\text{calories in 7 oz}}{7 \text{ oz}} \qquad \frac{\text{part}}{\text{whole}} = \frac{\text{part}}{\text{whole}}$$

   Step 2: Rewrite the word proportion with a variable and amounts from the problem.

   $$\frac{\rule{1cm}{0.4pt}}{2} = \frac{c}{7}$$

   Step 3: Solve the proportion.

   $$\frac{\rule{1cm}{0.4pt}}{2} = \frac{c}{7}$$

   $$\rule{1cm}{0.4pt} \times 7 = c \times 2$$

   $$c = \rule{1cm}{0.4pt}$$

   There are _____ calories in 7 oz of pasta.

2. The Golden Gate Bridge is 6,480 feet long, and its towers are 756 feet tall. For a movie, a designer is building a model that is 180 inches long. How tall should the towers on the model be?

   Step 1: Write a word proportion to show the problem.

   $$\frac{\text{Height of model towers}}{\text{Height of _____}} = \frac{\text{Length of model}}{\text{Length of _____}}$$

   Step 2: Replace the words with numbers and a variable.

   $$\frac{h}{\rule{1cm}{0.4pt} \text{ ft}} = \frac{\rule{1cm}{0.4pt} \text{ in.}}{\rule{1cm}{0.4pt} \text{ ft}}$$

   Step 3: Solve the proportion.

   $$\rule{1cm}{0.4pt} \times h = 180 \times \rule{1cm}{0.4pt}$$

   $$h = \rule{1cm}{0.4pt}$$

   THINK: The size of the model is given in inches, so h is in inches.

   So, the towers on the model should be _____ inches tall.

PRACTICE

Write a proportion, using amounts from the problem. Then solve.

3. A vegetable stand sells 3 lbs of green beans for $4. How much would 9 lbs of green beans cost?

   _____

   _____

4. A recipe that will make 2 cakes requires 3 lb of flour. How many pounds of flour would you use to make 7 cakes?

   _____

   _____

5. On a map, a distance of 5 cm represents 2 km. If a highway is 16.5 km long, how long will it be on the map?

   _____

   _____

6. At a garden center, 10 marigold seedlings cost $2.50. How much would 25 seedlings cost?

   _____

   _____

7. Joe read 20 pages of a book in 52 minutes. How long would you expect him to take to read 75 pages of the book?

   _____

   _____

8. If a model maker uses a scale in which 3 inches represents 10 feet, how long will his model of a 35-foot boat be?

   _____

   _____

• Solving Proportions

TEST-TAKING PRACTICE

Choose the best answer for each problem. In the answer section at the bottom of the page, fill in the box of your choice.

1. A farm stand sells 8 tomatoes for $2.25. Which of the following proportions could be used to find how much 20 tomatoes would cost?

   A $\dfrac{1}{2.25} = \dfrac{c}{20}$ C $\dfrac{8}{c} = \dfrac{20}{2.25}$

   B $\dfrac{8}{2.25} = \dfrac{20}{c}$ D $\dfrac{2.25}{8} = \dfrac{20}{c}$

2. A painter estimates that she uses 0.5 gal paint to cover 200 sq ft. Which proportion could be used to find how much paint she would use to cover 850 sq ft?

   J $\dfrac{0.5}{200} = \dfrac{850}{p}$ L $\dfrac{850}{0.5} = \dfrac{p}{200}$

   K $\dfrac{1}{p} = \dfrac{850}{200}$ M $\dfrac{0.5}{200} = \dfrac{p}{850}$

3. Every 3 hours, a factory produces 4 new lawnmowers. How many lawnmowers does the factory produce in a 24-hour day?

   A 4 C 24
   B 16 D 32

4. To make a model of a 30-ft tall building, a model maker used a scale of 5 ft : 2 in. How tall is the model?

   J 12 in. L 30 in.
   K 20 in. M 12 ft 5.

5. For every $100 collected from ticket sales, a singer receives $20. How much money will she receive if there are total ticket sales of $245?

   A $12.25 C $49.00
   B $40.00 D Not given

Write About It
Write a plan for solving the following problem. Then solve.

6. A landscaper figures that it takes a 50-lb bag of grass seed to seed one-half an acre of land. He needs to seed 12 acres of land. How many pounds of grass seed will he need?

   _____
   _____
   _____
   _____
   _____
   _____
   _____
   _____

---

1. A ☐ B ☐ C ☐ D ☐   4. J ☐ K ☐ L ☐ M ☐
2. J ☐ K ☐ L ☐ M ☐   5. A ☐ B ☐ C ☐ D ☐
3. A ☐ B ☐ C ☐ D ☐

● Solving Proportions

Chapter 7 L3

Using Unit Rates

You can use a unit rate to help you solve problems.

Example 1

Mr. Foley is traveling in Germany. When he exchanges currency, he gets 1.4 Deutsche Marks per dollar. At that exchange rate, how many Marks will Mr. Foley receive for $200?

A. Write a word proportion to show the problem.

$$\frac{1.4 \text{ Marks}}{1 \text{ dollar}} = \frac{\text{Marks Mr. Foley will receive}}{200 \text{ dollars}}$$

> The unit rate, 1.4 Marks per dollar, means $\frac{1.4 \text{ Marks}}{1 \text{ dollar}}$.

B. Replace the words with numbers and a variable, and solve.

$$\frac{1.4}{1} = \frac{m}{200}$$

$$m = 1.4 \times 200$$

So, $m = 280$

> Note that you can solve this problem simply by multiplying the amount of dollars by the unit rate.

Mr. Foley will receive 280 Marks for $200.

Example 2

When Mr. Foley goes to Italy, he exchanges $200 for Italian currency, receiving 370,000 lira. How many lira would Mr. Foley receive for $1,150?

A. Find the unit rate in lira per dollar.

$$\text{lira per dollar} = \frac{370,000 \text{ lira}}{200 \text{ dollars}}$$

Unit Rate = 1,850 lira per dollar

B. Multiply by the unit rate to solve.

$1,150 \times 1,850 = 2,127,500$

Mr. Foley would receive 2,127,500 lira for $1,150.

● Solving Proportions

GUIDED PRACTICE

1. Geraldine drives 456 miles and uses 12 gallons of gasoline. How many miles can she travel on a full tank of 17.5 gallons of gasoline?

    Step 1: Find the unit rate in miles per gallon.

    miles per gallon = $\dfrac{456}{12}$

    Unit rate = _____ miles per gallon

    Step 2: Multiply by the unit rate to solve.

    17.5 x _____ = _____

    She can travel _____ miles on a full tank.

2. Clark needs $425 worth of repair work for his car. When he works a 7-hour day, he earns $59.50. How many hours will Clark have to work to earn enough for the car repairs?

    Step 1: Find the unit rate in dollars per hour.

    dollars per hour = $59.50 ÷ _____

    Unit rate = $ _____ per hour

    Step 2: Use the unit rate to solve.

    THINK: The answer will be in hours, and the rate is in dollars per hour. I should *divide* the repair cost by the unit rate.

    425 ÷ _____ = _____

    Clark will have to work for _____ hours.

3. Linda buys $4\tfrac{1}{2}$ pounds of salmon for her restaurant. She pays a total of $23.40. Later the same day, she decides to buy another $2\tfrac{1}{2}$ pounds of salmon. How much will Linda pay for the $2\tfrac{1}{2}$ pounds?

    Step 1: Find the unit rate in dollars per pound.

    dollars per pound = $ _____ ÷ _____

    Unit rate = $ _____ per pound

    Step 2: Multiply by the unit rate to solve.

    $2\tfrac{1}{2}$ x _____ = _____

    Linda will pay $ _____ .

PRACTICE

Find the unit rate and solve.

4. An architect's model of a building is 18 inches tall. The actual building is 72 feet tall. A model of a 40-foot-long boat is built to the same scale. How long is the model?

5. A jeweler bought 14 ounces of silver and paid $58.80. He used $3\frac{1}{2}$ ounces of the silver for a bracelet. How much did the silver in the bracelet cost the jeweler?

6. In Mexico, Millen exchanged $40 for 248 pesos. The next day, she exchanged $90 for Mexican pesos. How many pesos did she receive?

7. Jack's car will travel 348 miles on a full tank of gasoline. The tank holds 12 gallons. How far can the car travel on 5 gallons of gasoline?

8. The O'Reilly's car used $2\frac{1}{2}$ gallons of gasoline on a 105-mile trip. How many more miles can they drive if they have 9 gallons of gasoline left in the tank?

9. The front door of a house is 7 feet tall. On a scale drawing of the house, the door is 2 inches tall. If the house is 28 feet tall, how many inches tall is it in the drawing?

• Solving Proportions

TEST-TAKING PRACTICE

Choose the best answer for each problem. In the answer section at the bottom of the page, fill in the box of your choice.

1. Mark's car travels 364 miles on 14 gallons of gas. Which expression shows how far the car will travel on 3 gallons of gasoline?

    A $14 \times \frac{364}{3}$

    B $\frac{14}{364} \times 3$

    C $3 \times \frac{364}{14}$

    D $14 \times 364 \times 3$

2. Tierry exchanges $65 for 312 French francs. What is the unit rate in francs per dollar?

    J   0.21 francs per dollar
    K   4.8 francs per dollar
    L   4.8 dollars per franc
    M   48 francs per dollar

3. Gerri works 35 hours a week, and is paid a total of $399 a week. If Gerri only works 24 hours one week, how much will she earn?

    A $125.40   C $581.90
    B $273.60   D   Not given

4. One U.S. dollar is worth 1,850 Italian lira. Debbie wants to buy a skirt that costs 90,650 lira. How many dollars does the skirt cost?

    J $15   L $77
    K $49   M $1,850

Write About It

Write a plan for solving the following problem. Then solve.

5. Gabe is driving across the United States, a trip of 2,496 miles. The first day he drives 384 miles in 8 hours. If Gabe drives at the same rate, how many hours of driving will it take him to cross the country?

_____
_____
_____
_____
_____
_____
_____
_____
_____
_____
_____
_____

1. A☐ B☐ C☐ D☐   3. A☐ B☐ C☐ D☐
2. J☐ K☐ L☐ M☐   4. J☐ K☐ L☐ M☐

● Solving Proportions

Making a Rate Graph

Showing information in a line graph can help you solve rate problems.

Example

A taxi driver charges $1.50 at the start of a trip. Each mile traveled costs $0.50. How much would it cost to take the cab 8 miles?

A. On the graph, mark the point (0, $1.50) to show the start of the trip.

B. Now, mark the point that shows how much it costs to take the cab 1 mile.

   THINK: The first mile costs $1.50 + $0.50 = $2.

   I should mark the point for (1, 2).

C. Draw a straight line between the two points, and extend it across the graph.

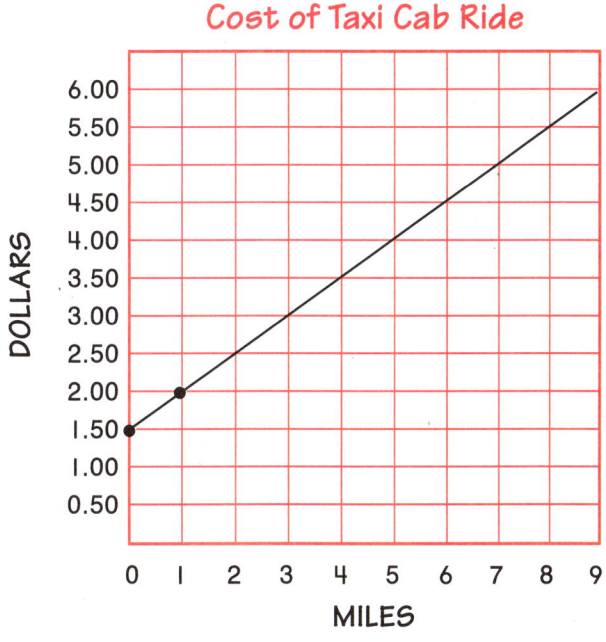

D. Use the line graph to find how much it would cost to take the cab 8 miles.

   Step 1: Move along the horizontal axis until you find 8 miles.

   Step 2: Move up to find the dollar amount on the vertical axis, and mark the point.

   What point shows the cost for 8 miles? (8, _____).

   So, it would cost $ _____ to take the cab 8 miles.

• Making and Reading Line Graphs

GUIDED PRACTICE

1. In another city, a taxi cab ride costs $2.00 at the start of the trip. Each $\frac{1}{2}$ mile traveled costs $0.25. How much does it cost to take a 4-mile ride?

   a. Label the vertical axis of the graph with dollar amounts in $0.25 intervals. (Hint: Start at $2.00.)

   b. Mark the point that shows the start of the trip.

   The point is (_____).

   Choose another point and graph it.

   For example, you could graph the point that shows how much the taxi costs after 1 mile. The point is (_____).

   c. Draw a straight line connecting the two points.

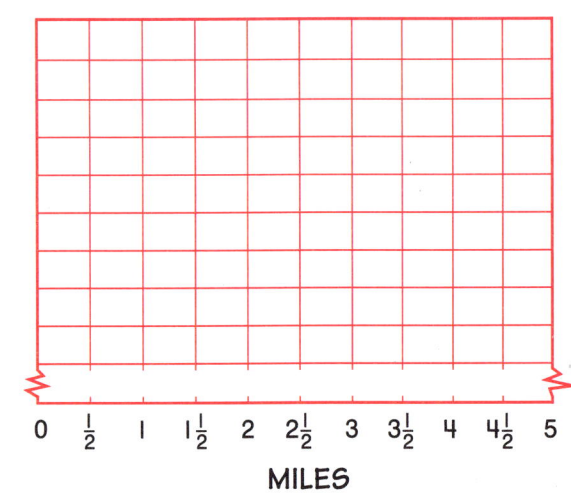

Cost of Taxi Cab Ride

   d. Use the line graph to solve the problem.

   What point shows the cost at 4 miles? _____

   It costs $ _____ to take a 4-mile cab ride.

You can use the line graph to solve other related problems.

2. How many miles could you travel for a cost of $3.25?

   What point shows a cost of $3.25? (_____)

   You could travel _____ miles.

108

PRACTICE

When Austin works as a baby-sitter, he receives carfare of $5, and $5 for each hour he baby-sits.

3. **Label the vertical axis of the graph below.**

4. **Draw two points, and complete the line graph.**

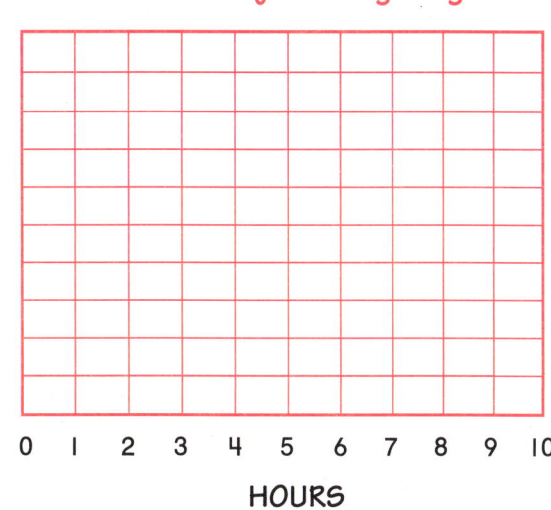

Use the completed line graph to solve.

5. **Austin baby-sat for 5 hours. How much money did he receive?**

   _____

6. **Austin baby-sat for 8 hours. How much money did he receive?**

   _____

7. **One day, Austin baby-sat for $9\frac{1}{2}$ hours. About how much money did he receive?**

   _____

8. **How many hours would Austin have to baby-sit in order to receive $35.00?**

   _____

• Making and Reading Line Graphs

TEST-TAKING PRACTICE
Choose the best answer for each problem. In the answer section at the bottom of the page, fill in the box of your choice.

The graph below shows the cost of rides at the school fair. The first ride costs $1. After that, each ride costs $0.50. Use the line graph to solve the problems.

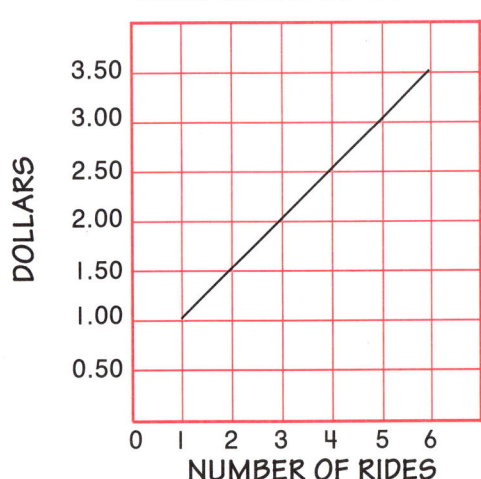

1. Which of the following points shows the cost of 3 rides at the school fair?
   A (0, 3.00)
   B (5, 3.00)
   C (3, 2.00)
   D (3, 2.50)

2. Which of the following points shows how many rides you can take for $3.50?
   J (6, 3.50)
   K (3.50, 6)
   L (6, 4.00)
   M (3.50, 5)

3. How many rides can you take for $1.50?
   A 1   C 3
   B 2   D 4

4. If you paid $2.50, how many rides could you take?
   J 1   L 3
   K 2   M 4

5. If you want to go on 5 rides, how much will you pay?
   A $2.50   C $3.50
   B $3.00   D Not given

Write About It

6. Does it cost exactly twice as much to take 4 rides as it does to take 2 rides? Explain your reasoning.

_____
_____
_____
_____
_____
_____
_____
_____

Chapter 8 L1

Using an Order Form

When you order merchandise, you often have to compute sales tax and shipping charges for your order. You can find the information that you need on the order form.

Example

Flora orders 2 pillows for $12.65 each, 2 sets of sheets for $24.00 each, and a set of pillow cases for $8.50. She wants the order delivered to her home in Massachusetts. Complete Flora's order, below.

Shipping and Handling		Order Form	
Orders Under $25.00 . . . add $5.00		Total Merchandise	$ _____
$25.01 to $75.00 . . . . add $8.00		For delivery in MA, add 5% sales tax.	$ _____
$75.01 to $150.00 . . . . . . add $11.00		Shipping	$ _____
$150.01 to $300.00 . . . . . add $12.50			
$300.01 and over . . . . . . add $14.00		Total	$ _____

A. Find the total price of the merchandise that Flora orders.

2 x $12.65 plus 2 x $24.00 plus $8.50 =   ?

$ _____ + $ _____ + $8.50 = $ _____

Complete the first line of the order form above.

B. Calculate the sales tax on Flora's order.

$ _____ x 5% =   ?

$ _____ x 0.05 = $ _____

Complete the second line of the order form above.

C. Use the table to find the shipping costs on Flora's order.

For an order of $ _____, the shipping is $ _____.

Complete the third line of the order form above.

D. Now add the cost of the merchandise, the sales tax, and the shipping charges.

$ _____ + $ _____ + $ _____ = $ _____

Complete the final line of the order form above.

• Percent of a Number

GUIDED PRACTICE

1. Complete the order form below.

   a. **Read along the first line of the order.**

   Which columns in this row include information you'll need?

   _____ and _____

   Multiply to calculate the Total Price for the row.   2 x $11.90 = $ _____

   Enter the amount on the form.

   b. **Use the same process for the other rows.**

Page	Style	Quantity	Size	Color	Description	Price	Total Price
6	32-7X	2	XL	red	T-shirts	$11.90	
21	41-2A	1	9	black	sneakers	$32.40	
14	17-6R	3	M	white	socks	$2.50	

2. If an order is sent to Vermont, sales tax of 7% must be added. How much will the sales tax in Vermont be for the order above?

   a. **Add to find the total cost of the merchandise.**

   _____ + _____ + _____ = _____

   b. **Multiply the total by the sales tax percent.**

   _____ x 0.07 = _____

   > When sales tax is not a whole number, round up to the next whole penny.

3. Use the amounts you have found for problems 1–2 and the table of shipping costs to complete the form below.

   Shipping and Handling

   Orders Under $20.00..... add $4.25
   $20.01 to $60.00......... add $6.00
   $60.01 to $100.00........ add $7.40
   $100.01 and over........ add $8.50

Total Merchandise	$ _____
In VT, add 7% sales tax.	$ _____
Shipping	$ _____
Total	$ _____

   a. **Fill in the price for Total Merchandise, from problem 1.**

   Now find the shipping costs for that amount in the table.

   Fill in the sales tax and the shipping costs from problem 2.

   b. **Add the amounts.**   _____ + _____ + _____ = _____

   Complete the final line of the order form.

PRACTICE

Complete each order form below. Compute the sales tax, use the table of shipping costs, and find the total amount of the order. When computing sales tax, round up to the nearest cent.

Shipping and Handling

Total Merchandise	Under $25.00	$25.01 to $50.00	$50.01 to $75.00	$75.01 to $100.00	$100.01 and over
Shipping Cost	$5.40	$7.80	$9.60	$10.90	$12.50

4.

Total Merchandise	$110.56
Add 7% sales tax.	
Shipping	
Total	

5.

Total Merchandise	$68.98
Add 8% sales tax.	
Shipping	
Total	

6.

Total Merchandise	$48.27
Add 4.5% sales tax.	
Shipping	
Total	

7.

Total Merchandise	$13.06
Add 6% sales tax.	
Shipping	
Total	

8.

Total Merchandise	$71.49
Add 3% sales tax.	
Shipping	
Total	

9.

Total Merchandise	$99.99
Add 6.5% sales tax.	
Shipping	
Total	

• Percent of a Number

TEST-TAKING PRACTICE

Choose the best answer for each problem. Where needed, use the table of shipping costs on the right. Fill in the answer box of your choice in the section at the bottom of the page.

Shipping and Handling

Under $25.00 . . . . add $4.50
$25.01 to $75.00 . . . . add $7.00
$75.01 to $150.00 . . . . . . add $10.25
$150.01 to $300.00 . . . . . add $11.75
$300.01 and over . . . . . . add $13.00

1. Ruth orders three lamps that cost $14.75 each. What is the cost of shipping for Ruth's order?
   - A $4.50
   - B $7.00
   - C $10.25
   - D $52.45

2. Thomas orders two CDs for $9.95 each and a third CD for $12.60. Which word equation can be used to find the total cost?
   - J $12.60 plus twice $9.95 = Cost
   - K Cost = $9.95 plus twice $12.60
   - L Cost = $12.60 minus $9.95
   - M Twice Cost = $12.60 plus $9.95

3. Ursula orders a modem for $145.00 and a telephone for $79.80. She pays shipping charges and 8% sales tax. What is her total cost?
   - A $236.55
   - B $242.79
   - C $254.54
   - D $255.68

4. Sue orders a bookcase for $275 and a table for $169. She pays shipping charges and 6.5% sales tax. What is the total cost of Sue's order?
   - J $444.00
   - K $457.00
   - L $472.86
   - M $485.86

5. Julio pays shipping charges but no tax on an order for two shirts that cost $29.95 each and a sweater that costs $44.50. What is his total cost?
   - A $104.40
   - B $114.65
   - C $116.15
   - D Not given

Write About It

6. If you were ordering two items that cost $100.00 each, would it be cheaper to order them together or in separate orders? Explain.

_____

_____

_____

_____

_____

_____

_____

1. A ☐ B ☐ C ☐ D ☐
2. J ☐ K ☐ L ☐ M ☐
3. A ☐ B ☐ C ☐ D ☐
4. J ☐ K ☐ L ☐ M ☐
5. A ☐ B ☐ C ☐ D ☐

• Percent of a Number

Percents, Fractions, and Decimals

Renaming a percent as a fraction or a decimal may make solving a percent problem easier.

Percents, Equivalent Decimals, and Fractions

1%	2%	4%	5%	10%	12.5%	15%	20%	25%	30%	$33\frac{1}{3}$%
0.01	0.02	0.04	0.05	0.1	0.125	0.15	0.2	0.25	0.3	0.333
$\frac{1}{100}$	$\frac{1}{50}$	$\frac{1}{25}$	$\frac{1}{20}$	$\frac{1}{10}$	$\frac{1}{8}$	$\frac{3}{20}$	$\frac{1}{5}$	$\frac{1}{4}$	$\frac{3}{10}$	$\frac{1}{3}$
37.5%	40%	50%	60%	62.5%	$66\frac{2}{3}$%	70%	75%	80%	87.5%	90%
0.375	0.4	0.5	0.6	0.625	0.667	0.7	0.75	0.8	0.875	0.9
$\frac{3}{8}$	$\frac{2}{5}$	$\frac{1}{2}$	$\frac{3}{5}$	$\frac{5}{8}$	$\frac{2}{3}$	$\frac{7}{10}$	$\frac{3}{4}$	$\frac{4}{5}$	$\frac{7}{8}$	$\frac{9}{10}$

Example 1

A fruit punch is 12.5% orange juice. How many ounces of orange juice are there in 40 ounces of the punch?

- **Decide what you need to find.** The solution will be 12.5% of 40 oz.

Step 1: Find the decimal and fraction equivalents of 12.5%.

12.5% is the same as 0.125 or $\frac{1}{8}$

Step 2: Solve the problem using the equivalents.

0.125 x 40 = 5 $\frac{1}{8}$ x 40 = 5

So, there are 5 oz of orange juice in 40 oz of punch.

> THINK: Using the fraction was easier, because 8 is a factor of 40.

Example 2

A newspaper reported that 60% of the 2,110 voters in town would vote for Green. How many people would vote for Green?

- **Decide what you need to find.** The solution will be 60% of 2,110.

Step 1: Find the decimal and fraction equivalents of 60%.

60% is the same as 0.6 or $\frac{3}{5}$.

Step 2: Solve the problem using the equivalents.

0.6 x 2,110 = 1,266 $\frac{3}{5}$ x 2,110 = 1,266

So, _____ people would vote for Green.

> THINK: Using the decimal was easier than using the fraction.

• Renaming Percents as Decimals and Fractions

GUIDED PRACTICE

1. A pair of shoes is marked down 30%. How much would you save from the original price of $60.00?

   a. What do you need to find?   30% of _____

   Find the decimal and fraction equivalents of 30%.

   30% is the same as _____ or _____.

   b. Choose either the decimal or the fraction and solve.

   _____ or _____

   You would save $ _____.

2. 87.5% of the 800 students at a school take the bus to school. How many students take the bus?

   a. What do you need to find?   87.5% of _____

   Find the decimal and fraction equivalents of 87.5%.

   87.5% is the same as _____.

   b. Choose either the decimal or the fraction and solve.

   _____

   So, _____ students take the bus.

3. George likes to tip 15% on his checks at restaurants. How much would he tip on a check for $40?

   a. What do you need to find? _____ of _____

   Find the decimal and fraction equivalents of 15%.

   15% is the same as _____ or _____.

   b. Choose either the decimal or the fraction and solve.

   _____

   George would tip _____.

4. For which of the problems on this page did you use a decimal? For which of the problems did you use a fraction? Explain your choices.

   _____

   _____

   _____

PRACTICE

Use the table of equivalent percents, decimals and fractions to help you solve each problem. Show the equations that you use.

Percents, Equivalent Decimals, and Fractions

1%	2%	4%	5%	10%	12.5%	15%	20%	25%	30%	$33\frac{1}{3}$%
0.01	0.02	0.04	0.05	0.1	0.125	0.15	0.2	0.25	0.3	0.333
$\frac{1}{100}$	$\frac{1}{50}$	$\frac{1}{25}$	$\frac{1}{20}$	$\frac{1}{10}$	$\frac{1}{8}$	$\frac{3}{20}$	$\frac{1}{5}$	$\frac{1}{4}$	$\frac{3}{10}$	$\frac{1}{3}$
37.5%	40%	50%	60%	62.5%	$66\frac{2}{3}$%	70%	75%	80%	87.5%	90%
0.375	0.4	0.5	0.6	0.625	0.667	0.7	0.75	0.8	0.875	0.9
$\frac{3}{8}$	$\frac{2}{5}$	$\frac{1}{2}$	$\frac{3}{5}$	$\frac{5}{8}$	$\frac{2}{3}$	$\frac{7}{10}$	$\frac{3}{4}$	$\frac{4}{5}$	$\frac{7}{8}$	$\frac{9}{10}$

5. Mary wanted a $160 coat, and waited until it went on sale for 25% off. How much does Mary save on the coat?

6. A chemist mixed a 200-mL solution so that it was 5% acid. How many mL of acid are in the solution he mixed?

7. A company increased its workforce by 75%. If the company originally employed 88 workers, how many new workers did it hire?

8. Sales tax in Alabama is 4%. How much sales tax would you have to pay if you purchased a car that cost $25,000?

9. At a town meeting, 40% of the people present voted in favor of building a new park. If there were 120 people present, how many voted for the park?

10. A sports announcer calculated that 37.5% of the cars on a racetrack were red. If there were a total of 48 cars on the track, how many of them were red?

• Renaming Percents as Decimals and Fractions

TEST-TAKING PRACTICE

Choose the best answer for each problem. You can use the chart of equivalents on the previous page. In the answer section at the bottom of this page, fill in the box of your choice.

1. Which number sentence can be used to find 62.5% of 800?

    A 6.25 x 800 = ?   C $\frac{3}{5}$ x 800 = ?

    B 0.625 x 80 = ?   D $\frac{5}{8}$ x 800 = ?

2. Harry is buying a bookcase originally priced at $200 that is marked down 40%. Which number sentence can be used to find how much Harry saves on the bookcase?

    J 0.04 x 200 = ?   L $\frac{40}{10}$ x 200 = ?

    K 0.4 x 200 = ?   M $\frac{4}{100}$ x 200 = ?

3. Sales tax in Arizona is 5%. How much sales tax would you have to pay on a purchase of $60?

    A $0.30   C $8.00
    B $3.00   D $15.00

4. At one school, 90% of the students preferred to start and finish the school day earlier. If there were 330 students in the school, how many of them preferred to start school earlier?

    J 33 students   L 297 students
    K 270 students   M 300 students

5. Which number sentence can be used to find 12.5% of 80%?

    A $\frac{1}{8}$ x 80% = ?   C 0.8 x 0.8 = ?

    B 0.125 x 0.08 = ?   D 8% x $\frac{4}{5}$ = ?

6. When a metal pipe was heated, its length increased by 4%. If the pipe was originally 250 cm long, by how many centimeters did its length increase?

    J 1 cm
    K 10 cm
    L 100 cm
    M Not given

Write About It

7. Write a percent problem that could be solved most easily either by using an equivalent decimal or by using an equivalent fraction. Then show how you would solve the problem.

    _____
    _____
    _____
    _____
    _____
    _____
    _____
    _____

---

1. A ☐ B ☐ C ☐ D ☐   4. J ☐ K ☐ L ☐ M ☐
2. J ☐ K ☐ L ☐ M ☐   5. A ☐ B ☐ C ☐ D ☐
3. A ☐ B ☐ C ☐ D ☐   6. J ☐ K ☐ L ☐ M ☐

● Renaming Percents as Decimals and Fractions

Chapter 8 L3

Writing Percent Equations

Many percent problems can be solved more easily by restating the problem to match this equation: *Whole x Percent = Part*.

Example 1

In a survey, 35% of the people said that they wanted new street lights in their town. If there were 660 people in the survey, how many of them wanted new street lights?

Step 1: **Write the percent equation.**

Whole x Percent = Part

THINK: The *Whole* is the 660 people surveyed.
The *Percent* is 35%.
I need to find the *Part*.

Step 2: **Substitute the known values in the equation.**

660 x 35% = p

Step 3: **Solve the equation for p.**

660 x 0.35 = 231

So, _____ people wanted new street lights.

Example 2

In a survey, 46% of the people said they did not want a new school. If there were 598 people who didn't want the school, how many people were surveyed?

Step 1: **Write the percent equation.**

Whole x Percent = Part

THINK: The *Percent* is 46%.
The *Part* is 598 people.
I need to find the *Whole*.

Step 2: **Substitute the known values in the equation.**

n x 46% = 598

Step 3: **Solve the equation for n.**

n x 0.46 = 598, so n = 598 ÷ 0.46

n = 1,300

So, _____ people were surveyed.

• Renaming Percents as Decimals

GUIDED PRACTICE

1. When 2,500 people were surveyed, 1,800 of them said that they would vote for Hillman. What percent of those surveyed planned to vote for Hillman?

   a. Write the percent equation.

   Whole x Percent = Part

   THINK: The *Whole* is 2,500 people.

   　　　　The *Part* is 1,800 people.

   　　　　I need to find the *Percent*.

   b. Substitute the known values in the equation.

   _____

   c. Solve the equation for n.

   2,500 x n = 1,800, so n = 1,800 ÷ 2,500 = 0.72

   0.72 is 72 hundredths, or 72%.

   So, _____ of those surveyed planned to vote for Hillman.

2. At the store where he works, Ned gets an employee discount of 12%. He saved $19.20 on a suit that he bought at the store. What was the original price of the suit?

   a. Write the percent equation.

   Whole x Percent = Part

   THINK: The *Percent* is _____.

   　　　　The *Part* is _____.

   　　　　I need to find the *Whole*.

   b. Substitute the known values in the equation.

   _____ x _____ = _____

   c. Solve the equation for n.

   n x 0.12 = $19.20, so n = _____ ÷ _____

   n = _____

   So, the original price of the suit was _____ .

Chapter 8 | **L3**

PRACTICE

Use the equation *Whole x Percent = Part* to solve each problem. Show your work.

3. An $84.00 computer game is marked down 25%. How much is taken off the price of the game?

4. Beth got a $7.20 discount on a book that originally cost $48. What percent was the discount?

5. Karin got a 10% discount on a washing machine, saving $28.00. What was the original price of the washing machine?

6. In a survey of 480 people, 24 people said they would vote for higher taxes. What percent of those surveyed would vote for higher taxes?

7. A watch that originally cost $48 is on sale for 20% off. How much is the price of the watch reduced?

8. The sales tax on a couch was $20.40. Sales tax is 6%. What was the price of the couch?

9. Noel spent $23.80 on school supplies. Sales tax is 7%. How much tax did he pay?

10. Of 2,456 students, 614 voted to change the school lunch program. What percent of the students voted for the change?

● Renaming Percents as Decimals

TEST-TAKING PRACTICE

Choose the best answer for each problem. In the answer section at the bottom of this page, fill in the box of your choice.

1. Larry received a 5% discount on a television, saving $23. Which equation can be used to find the original price of the television?
   A $n \times 23 = 0.05$
   B $23 \times 0.05 = n$
   C $n \times 23 \times 0.05 = 0$
   D $n \times 0.05 = 23$

2. When 850 people were surveyed, 476 of them said *No*. Which equation can be used to find the percent who said *No*?
   J $n \times 476 = 850$
   K $850 \times n = 476$
   L $476 \times 850 = n$
   M $476 \times n = 850$

3. At Clara's school, 36% of the students are vegetarians. If 504 students are vegetarians, how many students are there in the school?
   A 140 students
   B 181 students
   C 1,400 students
   D Not given

4. Josh buys a $1,600 laptop computer that is marked down 45%. By how much money is the price of the computer reduced?
   J $720
   K $880
   L $1,555
   M $3,555.55

5. Mary bought a vacuum cleaner that was marked $320. The salesperson gave her a $48 discount. By what percent was the price reduced?
   A 8%
   B 15%
   C 30%
   D 150%

6. In a survey, 75% of the people were not students. If there were 10,875 people who were not students, how many people were surveyed?
   J 8,156 people
   K 10,875 people
   L 14,500 people
   M 19,031 people

Write About It

7. Write a percent problem that asks what percent an amount is reduced. Then show how you would solve the problem.

_____
_____
_____
_____
_____
_____
_____
_____
_____
_____

1. A ☐ B ☐ C ☐ D ☐
2. J ☐ K ☐ L ☐ M ☐
3. A ☐ B ☐ C ☐ D ☐
4. J ☐ K ☐ L ☐ M ☐
5. A ☐ B ☐ C ☐ D ☐
6. J ☐ K ☐ L ☐ M ☐

• Renaming Percents as Decimals

Estimating Percents

Some problems ask you to estimate with percents. Estimating is also a good way to check that your answers to percent problems are reasonable.

Example 1

Julian wanted to buy a $240 stereo that was on sale for 35% off the listed price. By about how much was the price reduced?

A. **Decide what you need to find.**

THINK: I need to find 35% of $240.

Find a useful equivalent to 35%.

35% is a little more than $33\frac{1}{3}\%$, which is $\frac{1}{3}$.

B. **Use the equivalent to estimate.**

$240 \times 35\% = n$

$240 \times \frac{1}{3} \approx 80$

The price was reduced by about _____.

Example 2

Martha saved about $3.00 on a book that was marked down 22%. About how much did the book cost originally?

A. **Decide what you need to find.**

THINK: I need to find the amount that $3.00 is 22% of.

Find a useful equivalent to 22%.

22% is almost 25%, which is $\frac{1}{4}$.

B. **Use the equivalent to estimate.**

$n \times 22\% = 3.00$

$n \times \frac{1}{4} \approx 3.00$

$n \approx 3.00 \times 4$ So, $n \approx 12.00$

The book originally cost about _____.

● Finding a Fraction of a Number

GUIDED PRACTICE

1. Complete the number line below by filling in the percents.

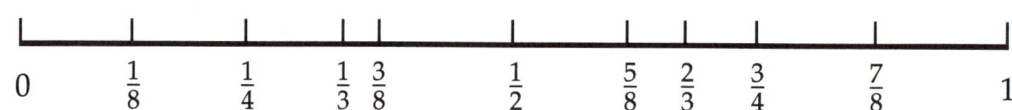

Use the number line to solve each problem.

2. Nadia saved $45 on a television she bought on sale. If the television was marked down 14%, about how much did it originally cost?

   a. **Decide what you need to find.**

   THINK: I need to find the amount that $45 is 14% of.

   Find a useful equivalent to 14% on the number line.

   14 % is about _____.

   b. **Use the equivalent to estimate.**

   $n \times$ _____ ≈ 45

   $n \approx 45 \div$ _____

   $n \approx$ _____

   The television originally cost about $ _____.

3. The cost of oranges at a grocery store increased by 65% after a harsh winter. If the oranges originally cost $0.90 per pound, by about how much did the price increase per pound?

   a. **Decide what you need to find.**

   THINK: I need to find 65% of $0.90.

   Find a useful equivalent to 65% on the number line.

   65% is about _____.

   b. **Use the equivalent to estimate.**

   _____ $\times$ _____ $\approx n$

   $n \approx$ _____

   The price increased by about $ _____ per pound.

Chapter 8 | **L4**

PRACTICE

Estimate to solve. Show the equation and equivalent fraction that you use for each problem.

4. Last month, Jill saved 27% of her $820 paycheck. About how many dollars did she save?

   _____

   _____

5. The price of a scarf was reduced by 15%, a savings of $4.00. About how much was the scarf originally?

   _____

   _____

6. Aaron bought a vintage car for $24,000. About how much profit did he make if he sold the car for 78% more than he had paid?

   _____

   _____

7. The population of a town increased by 31%. If the population was originally 66,000, by about how many people did it increase?

   _____

   _____

8. Jake's math test score improved by 30 points over the last test, an increase of 53%. What was his approximate score in the last test?

   _____

   _____

9. The membership of a club increased by 48%. If the club started with 150 members, about how many new members joined?

   _____

   _____

10. In a survey, 770 people—about 85% of those surveyed—wanted the city to build a public swimming pool. About how many people were surveyed?

    _____

    _____

11. About 68% of the 270 audience members at a theater were under the age of 20. About how many of the audience were under the age of 20?

    _____

    _____

● Finding a Fraction of a Number

TEST-TAKING PRACTICE

Choose the best answer for each problem. In the answer section at the bottom of this page, fill in the box of your choice.

1. A car's price was reduced by 14%, and the buyer saved $1,200. Which equation can be used to estimate the original price of the car?
   A $n \times 1{,}200 = \frac{1}{8}$
   B $1{,}200 \times \frac{1}{8} = n$
   C $n \times \frac{1}{8} = 1{,}200$
   D $n = 1{,}200 \times \frac{1}{8}$

2. In a survey of 636 people, 32% wanted new roads. Which equation can be used to estimate the number of those surveyed who wanted new roads?
   J $n \times \frac{1}{3} = 636$
   K $636 \times \frac{1}{3} \times n = 100$
   L $n \times 636 = \frac{1}{3}$
   M $636 \times \frac{1}{3} = n$

3. Marsha saved 27% on a table that she bought on sale. If the regular price of the table was $240, about how much did Marsha save?
   A about $60   C about $120
   B about $85   D about $120

4. Ken saved $30 when he bought a stereo that was marked down 15%. About how much was the regular price of the stereo?
   J about $85   L about $240
   K about $120   M Not given

5. Peter spent 85% of the $400 he had saved on a new mountain bike. About how much did the bike cost?
   A about $315   C about $385
   B about $350   D about $485

6. Of the 330 people who visited a museum one day, 69% came to see a special exhibit. About how many people came to see the special exhibit?
   J about 70   L about 220
   K about 110   M about 270

Write About It

7. How could you find the approximate sale price of a $20 item that was reduced by 24%?

Solving Multi-Step Percent Problems

It takes more than one step to solve some percent problems. To get the right answer, you have to decide what to do first.

Example 1

The Nolans paid $120,000 for their house. They sold the house for 20% more than they had paid. For how much did the Nolans sell their house?

Step 1: **Decide what you need to know.** You need to know
- the price that the Nolans paid for the house
- the increase in the value of the house
- the price that the Nolans sold the house for

Step 2: **Decide what you need to find first.**

THINK: I need to find the increase in value before I find the sale price. I need to find 20% of $120,00.

$120,000 x 20% = $120,000 x 0.20 = $24,000

Step 3: **Decide what operation you should perform.**

THINK: The house sold for <u>more</u> money, so I should add.

$120,000 + $24,000 = $144,000

So, the Nolans sold the house for $144,000.

Example 2

A car was regularly priced at $16,000. After 9 months, the car was marked down 20%. What was the sale price on the car?

Step 1: **Decide what you need to know.** You need to know
- the original price of the car
- how much the price was marked down
- the sale price of the car

Step 2: **Decide what you need to find first.**

You need to find how much the car was marked down first. You need to find 20% of $16,000.

$16,000 x 20% = $16,000 x 0.20 = $3,200.

Step 3: **Decide what operation you should perform.**

The car sold for <u>less</u> money, so you should subtract.

$16,000 − $3,200 = $12,800.

So, the sale price on the car was $12,800.

● Percent of a Number

GUIDED PRACTICE

1. A store reduced the price of a sweater by 10%, and later reduced the sale price by a further 25%. If the sweater was originally priced at $40.00, what is its final price?

   Note: When there are 2 steps in a percent problem, you cannot combine them—do them one step at a time.

   a. **Plan what to do first.**

   THINK: First, I should subtract 10% from the sweater's price.

Regular Price	−	10% Discount	=	Sale Price
$40.00	−		=	

   b. **Decide what to do next.**

   THINK: I should subtract 25% from the sale price.

Sale Price	−	25% Discount	=	Final Price
$36.00	−		=	

   So, the final price is $ _____.

2. In the five years after it was published, a comic book increased in value 50%. During the next five years, its value dropped 50%. If the comic book originally cost $2.00, what was it worth ten years later?

   a. **Plan what to do first.**

   THINK: First, I should add 50% to the comic's price.

Original Price	+	50% Increase	=	Value after 5 years
$2.00	+		=	

   b. **Decide what to do next.**

   THINK: I should subtract 50% from the new value.

Value after 5 years	−	50% Decrease	=	Value After 10 years
$3.00	−		=	

   So, the comic is worth $ _____.

   THINK: Adding 50% to a number and then subtracting 50% from the new number won't give you the original number!

PRACTICE

Solve. Show your work for each problem.

3. Employees at a store get a 20% discount. How much would an employee pay for a coat regularly priced at $78.00?

4. Patty invested $2,400 and earned 7% interest on her savings. What is the current value of Patty's investment?

5. Gia bought a house for $125,000. Its value decreased by 15% and then increased by 20%. What is the curent value of the house?

6. Jodi bought a watch that was regularly priced at $46.00 at a discount of 10%. The sales tax was 5%. How much did Jodi pay in all?

7. The population of a town decreased by 16%. If the population was originally 35,700, how many people now live in the town?

8. A tree that was 2 meters tall was planted, and its height increased by 83%. What is the current height of the tree?

9. Maria bought a car for $10,500. After a year, the car was valued at 22% less than its original cost. What was the new value of the car?

10. A couch marked $320 goes on sale at a 25% discount. The sale price is then reduced by 15%. What is the new price of the couch?

- Percent of a Number

TEST-TAKING PRACTICE

Choose the best answer for each problem. In the answer section at the bottom of this page, fill in the box of your choice.

1. Joe bought a new stove at a discount of 12%. The stove was originally marked $176. Which equation shows the price that Joe paid for the stove?
   A $176 x 12 % = n
   B $176 + ($176 x 12%) = n
   C n x 12% = $176
   D $176 − ($176 x 12%) = n

2. The value of a house has increased 10% each year. If it was valued at $100,000 two years ago, what is the house's current value?
   J $81,000
   K $110,000
   L $120,000
   M $121,000

3. Tawana saved 32% on a stereo that she bought on sale. If the regular price of the stereo was $340, how much did Marsha pay?
   A $108.80
   B $231.20
   C $308.00
   D $448.80

4. The population of a town increased by 10% and then decreased by 16%. If the population was originally 220,500, what is it now?
   J 166,698
   K 203,742
   L 207,270
   M 281,358

5. Dorothy bought a $20 bracelet that was discounted by 5%. She then paid sales tax of 5% on her purchase. What was Dorothy's total bill?
   A $19.95
   B $20.00
   C $20.05
   D $22.05

6. A bookstore sells all of its books at an 18% discount. At what price would the store sell a book originally marked at $16.50?
   J $2.97
   K $16.32
   L $13.53
   M Not given

Write About It

7. If you increase a number by 10% and then decrease the new number by 10% will your answer be greater or less than the original number? Explain.

_____
_____
_____
_____
_____
_____

1. A☐ B☐ C☐ D☐
2. J☐ K☐ L☐ M☐
3. A☐ B☐ C☐ D☐
4. J☐ K☐ L☐ M☐
5. A☐ B☐ C☐ D☐
6. J☐ K☐ L☐ M☐

● Percent of a Number

Test-Taking Skill: Visualizing the Problem

If you have trouble understanding how to solve a problem, try to show the information in another way. Here are some ways you might show it.

- Make a drawing, number line, or other visual model.
- Write a word sentence or word proportion for the problem.
- Make a table to find a pattern.

Example 1

Of the 750,000 people watching television on Monday, 3 out of 5 people were watching "It's My World." How many people were watching "It's My World"?

A 3 **B** 300,000 **C** 450,000 **D** 1,250,000

For problems that use ratios, think about using a table or a word proportion.

Step 1: Write a proportion to show the problem.

$$\frac{3 \text{ people}}{5 \text{ people}} = \frac{\text{People watching "It's My World"}}{\text{_____ people}}$$

Step 2: Use your proportion to solve the problem.

$$\frac{3}{5} = \frac{n}{750,000} \qquad \text{So, } n = \text{_____}$$

The correct answer is _____.

Example 2

The melting point of mercury is ⁻39°C. The boiling point is 357°C. What is the difference between mercury's melting and boiling points?

Step 1: **Draw a number line.** One end of the line shows positive temperatures and the other end shows negative temperatures. Label 0 at the center of the line.

Step 2: Mark the melting point of mercury to the left of 0, and the boiling point to the right of 0.

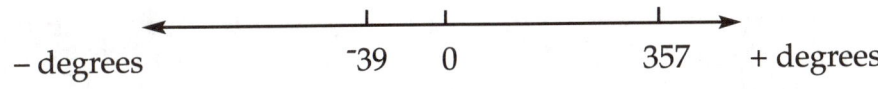

Step 3: Add the degrees between the melting point and 0 to the degrees between the boiling point and 0.   39 + 357 = 396

The difference between mercury's melting and boiling points is 396°C.

• Test-Taking Skill

TEST-TAKING PRACTICE

Choose the best answer for each problem. In the answer section at the bottom of the page, fill in the box of your choice.

1. A ferry boat charges $2 for the first passenger in a family, and $1.50 for each additional person. How much would a 6-person family pay?

    A $6.00   C $7.50
    B $6.50   D $9.50

2. George spent $8 on each of 2 T-shirts and $5.99 on socks, then bought lunch. He spent $26.40 in all. How much did he spend on lunch?

    J $4.41   L $21.99
    K $5.99   M $26.40

3. This morning, the temperature was ⁻4°F. By noon, the temperature was 8°F. By how many degrees did the temperature increase?

    A 4°F   C 12°F
    B 8°F   D 13°F

4. On the first play, the football team carried the ball forward 5 yd from the 20-yd line. On the second play, they were pushed back 7 yd. On what yard line is the ball now?

    J 18-yd line   L 25-yd line
    K 20-yd line   M 32-yd line

Use the calendar to solve problems 5-7.

APRIL						
SUN	MON	TUES	WED	THUR	FRI	SAT
				1	2	3
4	5	6	7	8	9	10
11	12	13	14	15	16	17
18	19	20	21	22	23	24
25	26	27	28	29	30	

5. What fraction of this month is either a Saturday or a Sunday?

    A $\frac{2}{15}$ C $\frac{8}{29}$
    B $\frac{4}{15}$ D $\frac{5}{30}$

6. Estimate what percent of the days of the year fall in April.

    J about 4%   L about 8%
    K about 5%   M about 30%

7. Today is April 19. A library book is due back at the library 3 weeks from the day Seth checked it out–12 days ago. What day is the book due at the library?

    A 21 days   C April 20
    B April 12   D April 28

1. A ☐ B ☐ C ☐ D ☐
2. J ☐ K ☐ L ☐ M ☐
3. A ☐ B ☐ C ☐ D ☐
4. J ☐ K ☐ L ☐ M ☐
5. A ☐ B ☐ C ☐ D ☐
6. J ☐ K ☐ L ☐ M ☐
7. A ☐ B ☐ C ☐ D ☐

• Test-Taking Skill

Choosing the Unit

Sometimes, you need to solve a measurement problem. You have to decide on the kind of answer you need. For example:

- Will the answer be an estimate or an exact answer?
- What kind of units will the answer need—linear units, square units, or cubic units?

Example

Suppose you want to tile the floor of the room shown at the right. To buy the tiles, each of which measures 1 foot x 1 ft, you need to know the area of the floor. What is the area?

10 ft

18 ft

A. **Decide on the kind of units you need.**

THINK: Area is given in square units.

The length and width of the floor are given in feet.

So, the area will be given in square _____.

> Length, width, and perimeter are given in linear units.
>
> Area is given in square units (units^2).
>
> Volume is given in cubic units (units^3).

B. **Decide whether to estimate or find an exact answer.**

THINK: To buy the correct number of tiles, you need an exact answer.

C. **Solve the problem. Find the area of the floor.**

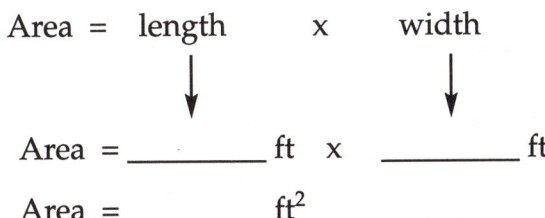

Area = length   x   width

Area = _____ ft x _____ ft

Area = _____ ft^2

The area of the floor is _____.

• Length, Area, and Volume

133

GUIDED PRACTICE

1. How many centimeter cubes can be shipped in the box shown at right?

   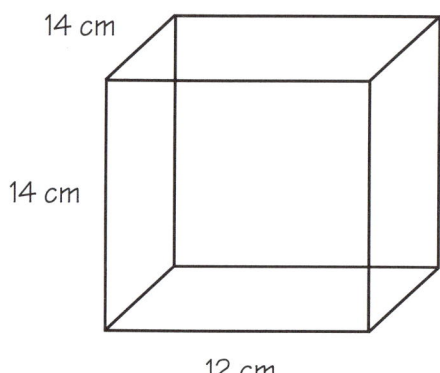

   Step 1: **Decide on the units you need.**

   The number of centimeter cubes that will fit in the box is the volume of the box. Which units will show the volume of the box?

   _____

   Step 2: **Decide whether to estimate or find an exact answer.**

   Do you need to find the exact number of cubes that will fit in the box, or will an estimate do?

   _____

   Step 3: **Find the volume of the box.**

   Volume = length × width × height

   Volume = _____ cm × _____ cm × _____ cm

   Volume = _____ cm³

   Step 4: **Decide what the final answer should be.**

   Read the problem question again. What will the answer show?

   _____

   So, _____ can be shipped in the box.

2. The school yard is 172 ft by 524 ft. The principal wants to fence the yard. How much fencing should she order?

   Step 1: **Decide on the kind of units the answer needs.**

   The length of the fence is the same as the _____ of the school yard.

   The answer will be in _____.

   Step 2: Do you need an exact number or an estimate? _____

   Step 3: **Estimate the perimeter of the school yard.**

   Round 172 to 200. Round 524 to _____.

   (2 × _____) + (2 × _____) = _____

   > Remember
   > P = (2 × l) + (2 × w)

   The principal should order about _____ ft of fencing.

134

PRACTICE

Decide on the kind of answer you need. Then solve.

Use the diagram at the right for problems 3–4.

3. Roy plans to fence a yard that is the length and width shown.

   a. How much fencing will Roy need?

   _____

   b. If the fence comes in 100-ft rolls, how many rolls will Roy need?

   _____

4. One bag of wildflower seed is enough to plant 400 square feet. Roy has 3 bags. **Does he have enough seed for his yard?**

   _____

Use the diagram at the right for problems 5–6.

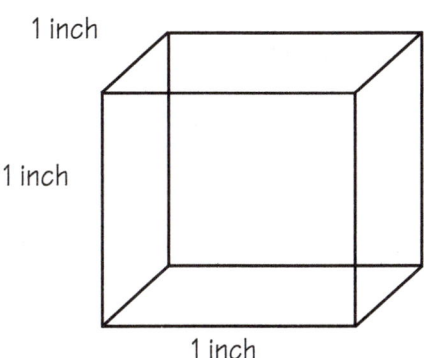

5. Jason made 1-inch blocks like the one shown for his nephew.

   a. What is the surface area of each block?

   _____

   b. Jason has a can of paint that will cover 100 square inches. How many blocks can he paint completely?

   _____

6. Jason has a shoe box that is 12 inches long, 6 inches wide, and 4 inches high. **How many 1-inch blocks can he pack into the box?**

   _____

7. A playground has the dimensions shown at right. Stella is planting tulips along the outside edges. **About how many feet around is the playground?**

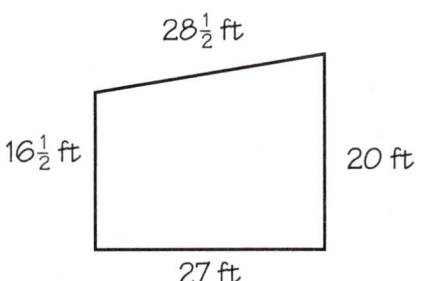

   _____

• Length, Area, and Volume

TEST-TAKING PRACTICE

Choose the best answer for each problem. In the answer section at the bottom of the page, fill in the box of your choice.

1. Claudia must find the area of a wall that is 8 ft high and 12 ft long. **In which units should the area of the wall be expressed?**
   A inches
   B cubic meters
   C feet
   D square feet

2. Which unit best describes the volume of a swimming pool?
   J cubic meters
   K square meters
   L meters
   M centimeters

3. Which estimate best shows the volume of the box below?

   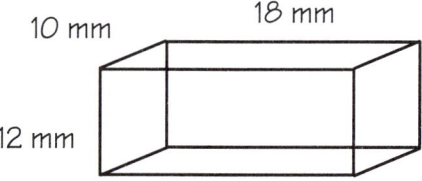

   A 40 mm   C 2,000 mm^3
   B 2,000 mm^2 D 4,000 mm^3

4. Armando has to fertilize a garden that is 12 ft long and 14 ft wide. Each bag of fertilizer covers 100 square feet. **How many bags of fertilizer should he buy?**
   J 1   L 3
   K 2   M 4

5. A field measures 325 ft by 800 ft. Its owner plans to fence the field. **How much fencing will it take?**
   A 1,125 ft   C 2,250 ft^2
   B 2,250 ft   D Not given

Write About It

6. How could you find how many square feet of wallpaper you need to cover the walls of a room?

Choosing the Formula

Sometimes, you may need to use a formula to solve a math problem. First, look at the variables in each formula to choose the right formula. Use numbers in the problem to replace variables in the formula. Then, you can solve for the variable that is the solution to the problem.

> **Formulas**
> Triangles:
> $A = \frac{1}{2} bh$
> $P = b_1 + b_2 + b_3$

Example

A triangular kite with a base of 6 ft has an area of 12 square feet. What is its height?

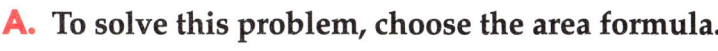 ← 6 ft →

A. **To solve this problem, choose the area formula.**

The formula for the area of a triangle is _____.

B. Look at the formula, $A = \frac{1}{2} bh$.

Write the values for the variables you know.

The kite has a base of 6 ft: $b =$ _____

The kite has an area of 12 square feet: $A =$ _____

> The letters used in your formulas will help you to remember what they stand for:
>
> A = area
> b = base
> h = height
> P = perimeter

C. **Rewrite the formula with the values you know.**

$A \quad = \quad \frac{1}{2} \quad \times \quad b \quad \times \quad h$

$\downarrow \qquad\qquad\qquad\qquad \downarrow$

_____ $= \quad \frac{1}{2} \quad \times \quad$ _____ $\times \quad h$

D. **Solve for h.**

$12 \quad = \quad \frac{1}{2} \quad \times \quad 6 \quad \times \quad h$

$\downarrow$

$12 \quad =$ _____ $\times \quad h$

Tip: You can write a related division problem to solve for h.

$12 = 3 \times h$ is the same as $h = 12 \div 3$.

$h = 12 \div 3$

$h =$ _____

The kite's height is _____ ft.

• Perimeter, Circumference, and Area

GUIDED PRACTICE

1. A bicycle tire covers a distance of 81.64 inches with each rotation. What is the diameter of the tire? Use 3.14 for π.

   > **FORMULAS**
   > **Area**
   > Circle: $A = \pi r^2$
   > Parallelogram: $A = bh$
   > Rectangle: $A = lw$
   > Triangle: $A = \frac{1}{2} bh$
   > **Circumference**
   > $C = \pi d \quad C = 2\pi r$
   > **Perimeter**
   > Rectangle: $P = (2l) + (2w)$

   Step 1: Decide which formula to use.

   THINK: Each rotation of a tire equals one circumference. To find the diameter of the tire, use the formula that has variables for circumference and diameter.

   The formula you need is _____.

   Step 2: Write the values for the variables you know.

   The circumference is 81.64 inches. So, C = _____.

   Step 3: Rewrite the formula with the values you know.

   C   = π x   d

   _____ =   _____   x   d

   Step 4: Solve for d.

   $d = 81.64 \div$ _____, so, $d =$ _____.

   The diameter of the bicycle tire is _____ inches.

2. A photograph has a perimeter of 24 inches. Each of the longer sides is 7 inches. What is the length of one of the shorter sides?

   Step 1: Decide which formula to use.

   A photograph is a rectangle. The formula for the perimeter of a rectangle is

   _____.

   Step 2: Rewrite the formula with the values you know.

   P   =   (2l)   +   (2w)

   _____ =   (2 x ___)   +   (2w)

   Step 3: Solve for w.

   $24 = (2 \times 7) + (2 \times w) \longrightarrow 24 =$ _____ $+ 2w$

   $2w = 24 -$ _____

   $w =$ _____ $\div 2$

   $w =$ _____

   The length of one of the shorter sides is _____ inches.

PRACTICE

Decide which formula you need. Then solve.

3. A rectangular house has a perimeter of 140 feet. If the house is 40 feet long, how wide is it?

   a. Write the formula you need to solve the problem.

   _____

   Solve. How wide is the house?

   _____

> **FORMULAS**
>
> **Area**
> Circle: $A = \pi r^2$
> Parallelogram: $A = bh$
> Rectangle: $A = lw$
> Triangle: $A = \frac{1}{2}bh$
> **Circumference**
> $C = \pi d$ $C = 2\pi r$
> **Perimeter**
> Rectangle: $P = (2l) + (2w)$

4. The piece of glass at the right is 80 centimeters long. Its area is 4,000 square centimeters. What is its height?

   a. Write the formula you need to solve the problem.

   _____

   b. Solve. What is the height of the piece of glass?

   _____

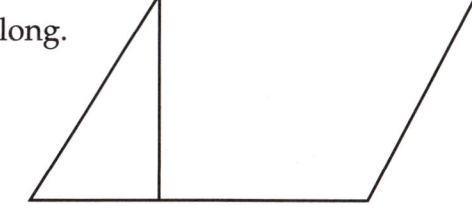

5. The circumference of a button measures $6\frac{2}{7}$ inches. What is its diameter? (Let $\pi = \frac{22}{7}$.)

   a. Write the formula you need to solve the problem.

   _____

   b. Solve. What is the diameter of the button?

   _____

6. The area of the flag at the right is 4,500 square centimeters. What is its height?

   a. Write the formula you need to solve the problem.

   _____

   b. Solve. What is the height of the flag? _____

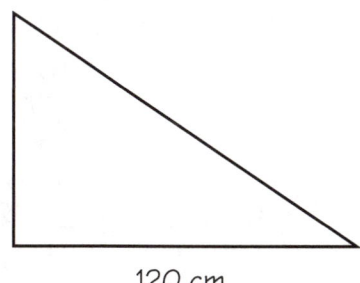

● Perimeter, Circumference, and Area

TEST-TAKING PRACTICE

Choose the best answer for each problem. In the answer section at the bottom of this page, fill in the box of your choice.

Formulas

Area	Circumference	Perimeter
Circle: $A = \pi r^2$ Parallelogram: $A = bh$ Rectangle: $A = lw$ Triangle: $A = \frac{1}{2}bh$	$C = \pi d \quad C = 2\pi r$	Rectangle: $P = (2l) + (2w)$

1. A circular window has a circumference of about 18 ft. What is its radius? Use 3.14 for π.

   Which of the following formulas could you use to solve the problem?
   A $C = \pi d$　　C $A = \pi r^2$
   B $C = 2\pi r$　　D $P = 2(l + w)$

2. The quilt piece below is a parallelogram that covers an area of 252 square centimeters. What is its height?

   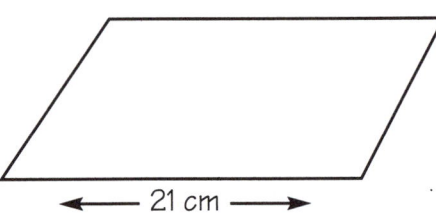

   J 6 cm　　L 10 cm
   K 8 cm　　M 12 cm

3. What diameter circle can be enclosed with 157 meters of fencing? Use 3.14 for π.
   A 25 m　　C 50 m
   B 40 m　　D 100 m

4. The field below has an area of 12,000 sq ft. What is its width?

   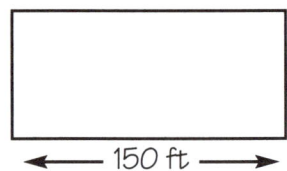

   J 40 ft　　L 230 ft
   K 80 ft　　M Not given

Write About It
Write a plan for solving the following problem. Then solve.

5. A triangular scarf has an area of 880 square inches. If it is 40 inches long, what is its height?

   _____
   _____
   _____
   _____
   _____
   _____

1. A ☐ B ☐ C ☐ D ☐　　4. J ☐ K ☐ L ☐ M ☐
2. J ☐ K ☐ L ☐ M ☐
3. A ☐ B ☐ C ☐ D ☐

● Perimeter, Circumference, and Area

Solving Multi-Step Problems

Sometimes, you need to use more than one formula to find the information you need to solve a problem. The first step is to write a word equation for what you need to find out.

Example

Mr. Everett put a circular fountain in his yard. He will plant grass in the rest of the yard. How many square feet of lawn will he have?

A. To solve this problem, you need to find the area of the yard that does not include the fountain. You can write a word equation to show what you need to find.

Area of the lawn = Total area of the yard – Area of the fountain

B. Decide which formulas you need.

THINK: The yard is a rectangle. Use the formula $A = lw$.

The fountain is a _____. Use the formula $A = \pi r^2$.

C. Solve the problem.

Step 1: Find the total area of the yard.

Total area = _____ x _____

Total area = _____ ft^2

Step 2: Find the area of the circular fountain. Let $\pi = 3.14$.

Area of fountain = 3.14 x _____^{2}

Area of fountain = _____ ft^2

Step 3: Place the areas you found in your word equation. Then solve.

Area of grass = Total area of the yard – Area of fountain

Area of grass = _____ ft^2 – _____ ft^2

Area of grass = _____ ft^2

Mr. Everett will have _____ square feet of lawn.

• Area, Circumference, and Volume

GUIDED PRACTICE

1. Ms. Webster is going to ship the smaller box inside the larger box. What volume will she need to fill with packing material?

   Step 1: Decide what you need to find.

   Need to find:
   The difference between the volume of the

   large box and the _____.

   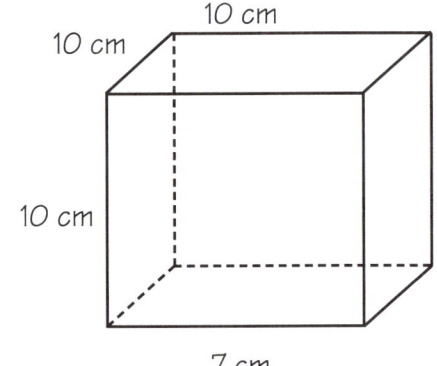

   Step 2: Write a word equation to show what you need to find.

   Volume to fill with packing =

   _____ − Volume of smaller box

   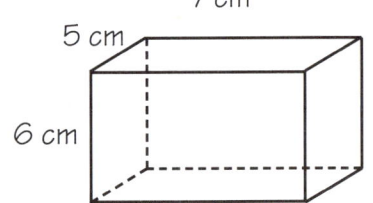

   Step 3: Decide which formulas you need.

   The larger box is a cube.

   Use the formula $V = $ _____.

   The smaller box is a rectangular prism.

   Use the formula $V = $ _____.

   FORMULAS

   Area
   Circle: $A = \pi r^2$
   Square: $A = s^2$
   Rectangle: $A = lw$
   Triangle: $A = \frac{1}{2} bh$
   Circumference
   $C = \pi d$ $C = 2\pi r$
   Volume
   Rectangular Prism:
   $V = lwh$
   Cube: $V = s^3$

   Step 4: Solve the problem.

   a. Find the volume of the larger box. Formulas

   Volume of larger box = _____

   Volume of larger box = _____

   b. Find the volume of the smaller box.

   Volume of smaller box = ____ × ____ × ____

   Volume of smaller box = _____

   c. Place the volumes you found in your word equation. Then solve.

Volume to fill with packing	**=**	**Volume of larger box**	**−**	**Volume of smaller box**
_____	=	_____	−	_____

   Ms. Webster will need to fill _____ with packing material.

Chapter 9 L3

PRACTICE

Decide which information you need to solve each problem. Then solve.

Area	Circumference	Volume
Circle: $A = \pi r^2$ Square: $A = s^2$ Rectangle: $A = lw$ Triangle: $A = \frac{1}{2}bh$	$C = \pi d \quad C = 2\pi r$	Rectangular Prism: $V = lwh$ Cube: $V = s^3$

Julia is paving the circular driveway, shown shaded at the right.

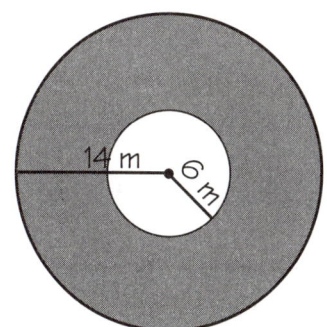

2. What is the driveway's area?

   a. Write a word equation to show what you need to find.

   _____

   _____

   b. Write the formula you need to solve the problem.

   _____

   c. Solve. Let $\pi = 3.14$.

   _____

Solve . . . .

The diagram at right shows Mr. Herrera's garden, made up of a half-circle and a square. Use the diagram for problems 3 and 4.

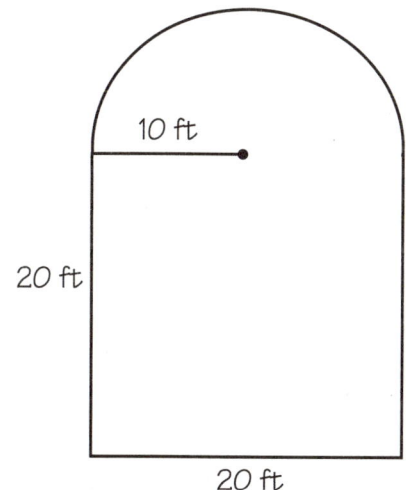

3. What is the distance around the garden?

   _____

4. What is the area of the garden?

   _____

• Area, Circumference, and Volume   143

TEST-TAKING PRACTICE

Choose the best answer for each problem. In the answer section at the bottom of this page, fill in the box of your choice.

1. What is the area of the shaded region?

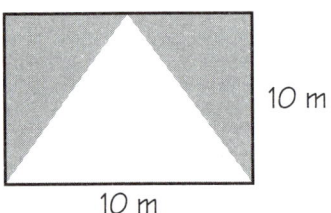

A 100 sq m   C 50 sq m
B 75 sq m   D 25 sq m

2. How much greater is the volume of the large box than the volume of the small box?

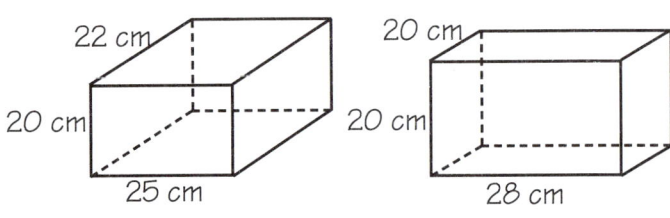

J 200 sq cm   L 1000 sq cm
K 800 sq cm   M 11,000 sq cm

3. Ms. Bismark wants to put lights around the pool shown. How many feet of lights does she need?

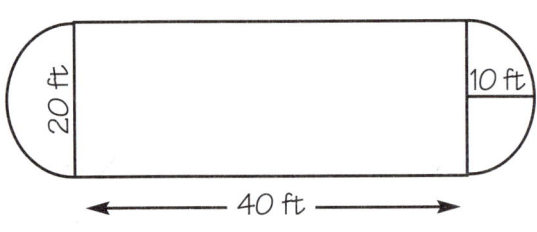

A 17.2 ft   C 142.8 ft
B 62.8 ft   D Not given

Write About It
Write a plan for solving the following problem. Then solve.

4. How many square feet of wall paper does Ms. Jones need to cover the wall shown below?

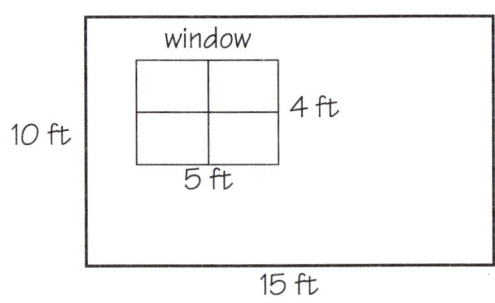

_____
_____
_____
_____
_____
_____
_____
_____
_____
_____
_____

1. A☐ B☐ C☐ D☐   3. A☐ B☐ C☐ D☐
2. J☐ K☐ L☐ M☐

Rewriting a Formula

Sometimes, you may need to show the information in a formula in another way to solve a problem. You may need to rewrite the formula.

Example

The area of the rug at the right is 96 sq ft. The rug is 8 ft wide. What is the length of the rug?

$w = 8$ ft $A = 96$ sq ft

$l = ?$

To solve this problem, you need to find the length.

A. First, decide which formula to use. Use what you know.

- You know that the **area** of the rug is _____ sq ft.
- You know that the **width** of the rug is _____ ft.
- You know that the rug is a **rectangle**.

Use the formula for the area of a rectangle: $A = lw$.

B. Rewrite the formula for area to solve for length.

THINK: Area = length × width $A = lw$

Length = _____ ÷ _____ $l =$ _____ ÷ _____

C. Rewrite the formula with the values you know and solve.

$$l = \frac{A}{w}$$

$l =$ _____

$l =$ _____

The length of the rug is _____ ft.

• Using Formulas

GUIDED PRACTICE

1. The circumference of a circular pool is 94.2 meters. What is the diameter of the pool? Use 3.14 for π.

    > **FORMULAS**
    >
    > **Area**
    > Circle: $A = \pi r^2$
    > Rectangle: $A = lw$
    >
    > **Circumference**
    > $C = \pi d$ $C = 2\pi r$
    >
    > **Perimeter**
    > Rectangle: $P = (2l) + (2w)$
    > Square: $P = 4s$

    Step 1: Use what you know.

    The _____ of the pool is 94.2 meters.

    Step 2: Decide what you need to find.

    the _____ of the pool.

    Step 3: Write the formula from the table to use.

    The formula for circumference of a circle, $C = \pi d$.

    Step 4: Rewrite the formula to solve for diameter. Then solve.

    $C = \pi d$

    $d = $ _____ ÷ _____

    $d = \dfrac{\text{_____}}{3.14}$

    $d = $ _____

    The diameter of the pool is _____ meters.

2. The perimeter of a square is 56 centimeters. What is the length of each of its sides?

    a. I know that the _____ of the square is 56 centimeters.

    b. I need to find the length of each _____.

    c. Write the formula to use.

    The formula for perimeter of a square, $P = 4s$.

    d. Solve.

    $P = 4s$

    $s = $ _____ ÷ _____

    $s = \dfrac{\text{_____}}{4}$

    $s = $ _____

    The perimeter of the square is _____ cm.

Chapter 9 **L4**

PRACTICE

Decide which formula to use. Rewrite the formula to solve for the missing value. Then solve.

> **FORMULAS**
>
> **Area**
> Circle: $A = \pi r^2$
> Parallelogram: $A = bh$
> Rectangle: $A = lw$
> Triangle: $A = \frac{1}{2}bh$
>
> **Circumference**
> $C = \pi d \quad C = 2\pi r$
>
> **Perimeter**
> Rectangle: $P = 2(l + w)$
> Square: $P = 4s$
>
> **Distance**
> $d = rt$

3. The circumference of a circular garden is 56.52 ft. What is the radius of the garden? (Let $\pi = 3.14$.)

   a. Write the formula you need to solve the problem.

   _____

   b. Rewrite the formula to solve for the radius.

   _____

   c. Solve.

   _____

4. Andrea drove 162 miles in 3 hours. What was her average speed (rate)?

   a. Write the formula you need to solve the problem. _____

   b. Rewrite the formula to solve for rate. _____

   c. Solve. Andrea's average speed was _____.

5. The carpet in Ed's living room covers 182 square feet. If the carpet is 14 feet long, what is the width of the carpet?

   a. Write the formula you need to solve the problem. _____

   b. Rewrite the formula to solve for width. _____

   c. Solve. The width of the carpet is _____.

6. The puzzle piece at right has an area of $8\frac{3}{4}$ square inches. How long is its base?

   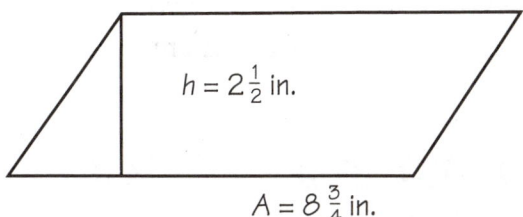

   a. Write the formula you need to solve the problem.

   _____

   b. Solve. The base of the puzzle is _____ long.

● Using Formulas

147

TEST-TAKING PRACTICE

Choose the best answer for each problem. In the answer section at the bottom of this page, fill in the box of your choice.

1. A circular rug has an area of 28.26 ft². What is its radius?

   The formula for the area of a circle is $A = \pi r^2$. Which of the following versions of the formula would be the best choice to solve the problem?
   A $A = \pi r^2$
   B $\pi = A/r^2$
   C $r^2 = A/\pi$
   D $r^2 = \pi/A$

2. Ms. Ortega plans to drive 500 miles at an average speed of 60 miles per hour. About how long will it take her to arrive at her destination?
   J about 8 hours
   K about 12 hours
   L about 15
   M about 11 hours

3. The room below has an area of 88 ft². What is the room's length?

   8 ft

   A 8 ft
   B 11 ft
   C 88 ft
   D 704 ft

4. A square has a perimeter of 16.4 cm. What is the length of one of its sides?
   J 65.6 cm
   K 32.8 cm
   L 8.2 cm
   M 4.1 cm

5. A tile in the shape of a parallelogram has a base of $4\frac{1}{2}$ inches. Its area is 27 in.². What is the tile's height?
   A 4 in.
   B 6 in.
   C 9 in.
   D Not given

Write About It

Write a plan for solving the following problem. Then solve.

6. A circular garden has a circumference of 34.54 ft. You want to build a straight path from the circle to its center. How long will the path be? (Use 3.14 for π.)

   _____
   _____
   _____
   _____
   _____
   _____
   _____
   _____
   _____
   _____

1. A ☐ B ☐ C ☐ D ☐
2. J ☐ K ☐ L ☐ M ☐
3. A ☐ B ☐ C ☐ D ☐
4. J ☐ K ☐ L ☐ M ☐
5. A ☐ B ☐ C ☐ D ☐

• Using Formulas

Chapter 10 | **L1**

Renaming Measures

To solve some problems, you have to compute with measurements that are given with unlike or mixed units. It's often helpful to change the measurements to a single unit first.

Example 1

Art has a board of wood that is 5 ft 6 in. long. He wants to cut it into 3 equal lengths. How long will each piece of wood be?

A. Decide how to rename the measure as a single unit.

To multiply or divide a measurement that is given in mixed units, it's usually easier to rename it, using the **smaller** units.

THINK: I can write the measurement as inches.

> When you solve problems with mixed units, you can
> - Rename measures with the smallest unit.
> - Rename measures with the largest unit.
> - Compute with the given units, and rename the result.

5 ft 6 in. = 5 ft + 6 in.   5 ft x 12 = 60 in.   60 in. + 6 in. = 66 in.

B. Compute, with the measurement written as a single unit.

66 in. ÷ 3 = 22 in., so each piece will be 22 in. long.

22 in. = 1 ft 10 in.

Each piece of wood will be 1 ft 10 in. long.

Example 2

It takes Jeff 1 minute 30 seconds to ride around the block. At that rate, how long will it take him to ride around the block 30 times?

A. Decide how to rename the measure as a single unit.

Sometimes, it's easier to use the **larger** units. In this multiplication problem, if the smaller unit (seconds) were used, the number of seconds would be very large. So, rename using minutes.

THINK: 30 seconds is exactly $\frac{1}{2}$ minute.

1 minute 30 seconds = _____.

B. Compute, with the measurement written as a single unit.

$1\frac{1}{2}$ minutes x 30 = 45 minutes

It will take Jeff 45 minutes to ride around the block 30 times.

• Multiplying and Dividing Mixed Numbers

GUIDED PRACTICE

1. Arden's puppy weighs 5 pounds 12 ounces, and Jed's puppy weighs 7 pounds 9 ounces. How much do the two puppies weigh together?

   a. Decide whether or not to rename the units.

   For some addition or subtraction problems, you may find it easiest to leave the mixed units as they are.

   b. Add like units, beginning with the smaller ones.

      5 lb 12 oz

   + 7 lb 9 oz

      12 lb 21 oz ⟶ 12 lb + 1 lb 5 oz ⟶ 13 lb 5 oz

   Together, the puppies weigh _____ lb _____ oz.

2. A tank contain 6 gallons 3 quarts of water. How many $\frac{3}{4}$-gallon containers can be filled from the tank?

   a. Decide whether or not to rename the units.

   THINK: When dividing, it's usually easiest to use small units. In this problem, I can change <u>both</u> measurements to quarts.

   (1) 6 gal ⟶ 6 x 4 ⟶ 24 qt

   So, 6 gal 3 qt ⟶ 24 + 3 ⟶ 27 qt.

   (2) $\frac{3}{4}$ gal = 3 qt

   b. Compute, using like units.

   27 qt ÷ 3 qt = _____

   So, _____ containers can be filled.

3. It takes 1 minute 48 seconds to fill a 1-gallon bucket. How long will it take to fill a 5-gallon bucket?

   a. Decide whether or not to rename the units.

   • Would you rename the units as minutes? _____

   • Would you rename the units as seconds? _____

   • Would you leave the units as minutes and seconds? _____

   b. Compute.

   5 x _____ = _____

   It will take _____ to fill a 5-gallon bucket.

Chapter 10 | **L1**

PRACTICE

Solve each problem, showing your work.

4. A machine takes 2 minutes 6 seconds to make a plate. How long will it take to make 10 plates?

5. A snail travels 3 ft 7 in. along a path, and then travels another 2 ft 10 in. How far does the snail travel?

6. A videotape of 7 episodes of a cartoon lasts for 2 hours 20 minutes. If each episode is the same length, how long does each episode last?

7. A cook cuts a piece of cheese weighing 2 lb 11 oz from a block weighing 7 lb 4 oz. How much does the block of cheese weigh now?

8. Jorge makes 4 gallons 1 quart of punch for his party. The glasses that he has each hold $\frac{1}{3}$ quart. How many glasses can Jorge fill with the punch that he has made?

9. During a commercial break on television, each advertisement lasts 20 seconds. If the break lasts 3 minutes 40 seconds, how many advertisements are shown?

● Multiplying and Dividing Mixed Numbers

TEST-TAKING PRACTICE

Choose the best answer for each problem. Fill in the answer box of your choice in the section at the bottom of this page.

1. Tami jumped 10 ft 9 in. on her first jump. Her second jump was 11 inches longer. Which expression shows the length of her second jump?
   A 10 ft + 9 in. − 1 ft + 1 in.
   B 10 ft + 1 ft 8 in.
   C 11 ft + 3 in. + 11 in.
   D 129 in. − 11 in.

2. Teresa poured 4 gal 3 qt of water into a tub that can hold 8 gal 1 qt. Which expression shows how much more water the tub will hold?
   J 12 gal + 1 gal
   K 4 gal + 2 qt
   L 33 qt − 19 qt
   M 33 qt + 19 qt

3. During the summer, it took Horace an average of 2 hr 12 minutes to mow his lawn. If he mowed the lawn 12 times, how long did he spend mowing?
   A 14 h 24 min
   B 16 h 24 min
   C 24 h 24 min
   D 26 h 24 min

4. Daud bought a box of glass beads weighing 7 lb 2 oz. He divided the beads into bags that each contained 6 oz. How many bags did he fill?
   J 12 bags
   K 16 bags
   L 19 bags
   M 22 bags

5. A room is 12 ft 3 in. long and 8 ft 10 in. wide. How much greater is the room's length than its width?
   A 3 ft 1 in.
   B 3 ft 5 in.
   C 4 ft 5 in.
   D Not given

Write About It

6. What is the area of a room that is 10 ft long and 8 ft 3 in. wide? Explain how you reached your solution.

___

1. A☐ B☐ C☐ D☐
2. J☐ K☐ L☐ M☐
3. A☐ B☐ C☐ D☐
4. J☐ K☐ L☐ M☐
5. A☐ B☐ C☐ D☐

• Multiplying and Dividing Mixed Numbers

Interpreting Remainders

In division problems with measurements, there is sometimes a remainder. Deciding what kind of answer makes sense lets you know what the remainder means.

Example

A plumber is cutting an 11-foot length of pipe into sections that are each $1\frac{1}{2}$ feet long. How many sections can the plumber cut, and how much will be leftover?

A. First divide the total length by the length of each section.

$11 \div 1\frac{1}{2} = 7\frac{1}{3}$.

Because you're dividing the total feet by the feet per section, the quotient is the number of sections.

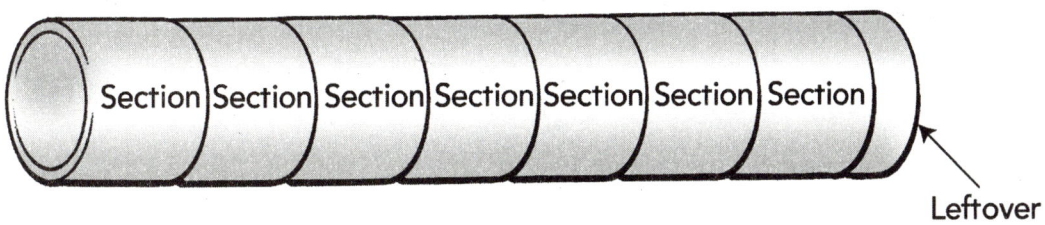

B. Decide what the remainder means.

THINK: The quotient is the number of sections, so the remainder is also given in number of sections.

There will be $\frac{1}{3}$ of a section left.

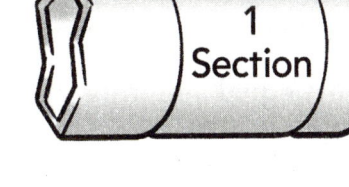

C. Use the remainder to find the length of pipe leftover.

Each section is $1\frac{1}{2}$ feet long.

So, $\frac{1}{3}$ section ⟶ $\frac{1}{3} \times 1\frac{1}{2}$ ft ⟶ $\frac{1}{2}$ ft ⟶ 6 in.

So, there will be _____ sections, and _____ inches of pipe leftover.

• Dividing Mixed Numbers

GUIDED PRACTICE

1. A block of cheese that weighs 3 lb 6 oz is divided into pieces that each weigh 4 oz. How many pieces are there, and how much cheese is leftover?

   a. Divide the weight of the block by the weight of the pieces.

   First, rename the units so that you can divide.

   3 lb 6 oz = 54 oz.   54 oz ÷ 4 oz = $13\frac{1}{2}$ pieces

   b. Decide what the remainder means.

   What are the units of the quotient? _____

   What are the units of the remainder? _____

   c. Use the remainder to find the amount of cheese leftover.

   Each piece weighs 4 oz, so $\frac{1}{2}$ piece weighs 4 oz x $\frac{1}{2}$ = _____

   So, there will be _____ pieces with _____ oz leftover.

2. A block of cheese that weighs 3 lb 6 oz is divided into 4 equal pieces. How much does each piece weigh?

   a. Divide the weight of the cheese by the number of pieces.

   First, change the units so that you can divide.

   3 lb 6 oz = 54 oz.   54 oz ÷ 4 = $13\frac{1}{2}$ oz

   b. Decide what the remainder means.

   What are the units of the quotient? _____

   What are the units of the remainder? _____

   So, each piece of cheese weighs _____ ounces.

3. Phil has a pitcher with 50 ounces of juice.

   a. If he pours equal amounts into 6 glasses, how much is in each glass?

   _____

   b. If he pours 6 ounces into each glasses, how many glasses can he fill?

   _____

PRACTICE

Solve each problem, showing your work.

4. A museum guide schedules 15 tours of a gallery of modern sculpture that is open for 8 hours. What is the longest a tour can last, if each tour is the same?

5. A cook has 6 lb 5 oz of prepared fish. He uses it to make 5-oz portions of fish for a recipe. How many portions can he make, and how much will be leftover?

6. A water cooler holds 8 gallons. If MaryBeth fills as many 6-quart jugs as she can from the water cooler, how much water will be left over?

7. Rory has a roll of green fabric that is 24 ft 6 in. long. If he cuts the fabric into 14 equal lengths, how long will each piece be?

8. The 108 students in the 6th grade at a school are assigned to work in groups of 7 people. How many students won't be in a complete group?

9. There are 221 students going on a school trip. How many buses do they need, if each bus can carry 42 passengers?

● Dividing Mixed Numbers

TEST-TAKING PRACTICE

Choose the best answer for each problem. Fill in the answer box of your choice in the section at the bottom of this page.

1. How many 7-oz hamburgers can a cook make from 5 lb 3 oz of meat?
   A 6 oz
   B 77 oz
   C 11 hamburgers
   D 12 hamburgers

2. A roll of wire that is 22 ft 6 in. long is cut into 9 equal pieces. How long is each piece?
   J $2\frac{1}{2}$ pieces
   K 2 ft 6 in.
   L 2 ft 9 in.
   M 18 ft

3. Cameron cuts as many 1-ft-9-in.-long shelves as he can from a board that is 12 ft long. How much wood will be leftover?
   A 1 ft 6 in.
   B 6 shelves
   C 7 shelves
   D 10 ft 3 in.

4. A librarian is packing 145 books into boxes that will each hold 24 books. How many boxes will she need to pack all of the books?
   J 1 book
   K 144 books
   L 6 boxes
   M 7 boxes

5. An album holds 32 photos. How many albums will 244 photos fill completely?
   A 7 albums   C 20 photos
   B 8 albums   D 224 photos

6. Malik records as many 25-second commercials as possible on a 30-minute tape. How much tape is leftover?
   J none   L 5 minutes
   K 20 seconds   M Not given

Write About It

7. Max cuts 4 pieces of pipe 1 ft 8 in. long and 3 pieces of pipe 1 ft 2 in. long from an 11-ft-6-in. length of pipe. Can she cut another piece—of either length—from what's left over? Explain how you can solve this problem.

_____
_____
_____
_____
_____
_____
_____
_____

1. A☐ B☐ C☐ D☐   4. J☐ K☐ L☐ M☐
2. J☐ K☐ L☐ M☐   5. A☐ B☐ C☐ D☐
3. A☐ B☐ C☐ D☐   6. J☐ K☐ L☐ M☐

● Dividing Mixed Numbers

Test-Taking Skill: Writing a Plan

On some tests you need to explain how to solve a problem. It is important to explain your thinking and show your calculations.

Example

The length of a cardboard box is 20 inches, and its height is 13 inches. The area of each end of the box is 143 square inches. What is the surface area of the entire box?

A. Read the problem and study the diagram. Decide what you need to know to solve the problem.

You need to know the length, width, and height of the box.

THINK: I don't know the width, but I <u>can</u> find it.

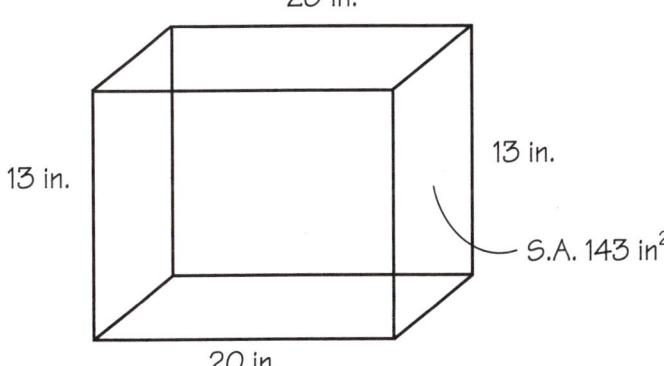

B. Make a plan. Write your plan.

Step 1: Use the area of the end of the box to find its width.

Step 2: Find the area of each face of the box.

Step 3: Find the sum of the areas of all the faces of the box.

C. Solve the problem, showing your calculations.

Step 1: Area of each end = $h \times w$ so, $143 = 13 \times w$ $w = 11$

Step 2: Area of each side = $l \times h$ $A = 20 \times 13 = 260$ in^2

Area of the top or the bottom = $l \times w = 20 \times 11 = 220$ in^2

Area of each end (given) = 143 in^2

Step 3: Surface area of box = $(2 \times 260) + (2 \times 220) + (2 \times 143)$

= 520 + 440 + 286 = 1,246 in^2

The surface area of the entire box is 1,246 square inches.

• Test-Taking Skill

TEST-TAKING PRACTICE

Make a plan to solve the problem. Then solve. Explain your thinking.

1. Ms. Noronha owns a pet store. She bought a puppy for $250, and priced it at 50% more than she paid. However, she decided to sell the puppy to a customer at 15% off the price. How much did she sell the puppy for?

2. A man visiting Canyonlands National Park in Utah stands facing a far-off cliff. He shouts out his name, and it takes 12 seconds for an echo to return to him. If sound travels at 1,088 feet/second, how many miles, to the nearest quarter mile, is the man from the cliff? (5,280 feet = 1 mile)

Drawing Pictures

You can solve some problems easily if you show the information another way, by drawing a picture.

Example 1

A box is 12 inches long, 10 inches wide, and 8 inches tall. How many 1-inch square stickers would it take to cover the box?

A. Draw a picture of the box.

Decide what you need to find.

THINK: The number of stickers will be the same as the surface area of the box in square inches.

B. Draw each face of the box so that you can find its surface area.

Label the drawings with the measurements.

THINK: There are 6 faces—3 pairs that have the same dimensions.

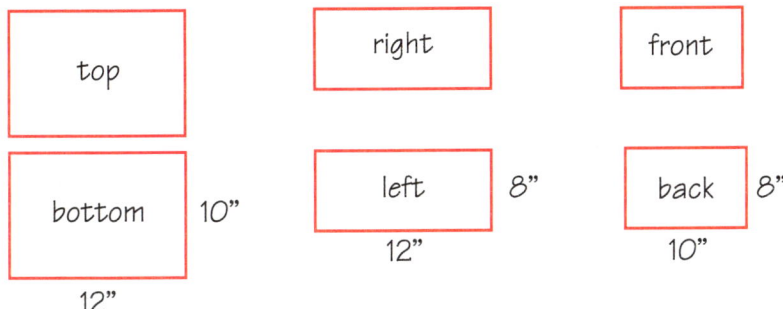

C. Find the area of each face of the box.

The area of the largest face = 12 x 10 = _____ sq in.

So the area of the 2 largest faces is _____ x 2 = _____ sq in.

The area of the middle face = 12 x 8 = _____ sq in.

So the area of the 2 middle faces is _____ x 2 = _____ sq in.

The area of the smallest face = 8 x 10 = _____ sq in.

So the area of the 2 smallest faces is _____ x 2 = _____ sq in.

D. Add the areas of the faces to find the total surface area of the box.

_____ + _____ + _____ = _____ sq in.

Each sticker covers 1 square inch.

So, it would take _____ stickers to cover the box.

• Areas of Rectangles, Circles, and Triangles

GUIDED PRACTICE

1. A roofer charges by the square foot. How many square feet of roofing are needed for the roof shown at the right, including the triangular ends.

   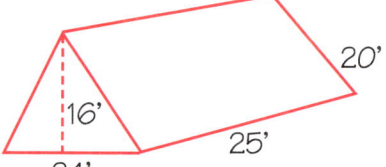

   a. Draw each face of the roof. Label the dimensions of the different faces.

   b. Find the area of each face.

   The area of each rectangular face = l x w

   A = _____ ft x _____ ft = _____ sq ft

   Find the area of the two rectangular faces.

   2 x _____ = _____ sq ft

   The area of each triangular face = $\frac{1}{2}bh$

   A = $\frac{1}{2}$ x _____ ft x _____ ft = _____ sq ft

   Find the area of the two triangular faces.

   2 x _____ = _____ sq ft

   c. Add to find the total area.

   _____ + _____ = _____ sq ft

   So, the area of the roof is _____ sq ft.

   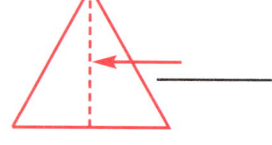

2. A cylindrical drum has a radius of 7 in. and a height of 30 in. What is its surface area? (Use $\pi = \frac{22}{7}$)

   a. Draw each surface.

   b. Find the area of each circular surface.

   A = πr^2 = $\frac{22}{7}$ x 7 x 7 = _____ sq in.

   Find the area of the two circles.

   2 x _____ = _____ sq in.

   c. Find the area of the rectangle.

   THINK: The length of the rectangle is the circumference of the circles.

   C = $2\pi r$ = 2 x $\frac{22}{7}$ x 7 = _____ in.

   A = l x w ⟶ C x w = _____ x _____ ⟶ A = _____ sq in.

   d. Add to find the total surface area.

   _____ + _____ = _____ sq in.

   So, the surface area of the drum is _____ sq in.

160

PRACTICE

Use the diagram of a building that is being renovated to solve the problems. You may want to draw pictures on a separate sheet of paper.

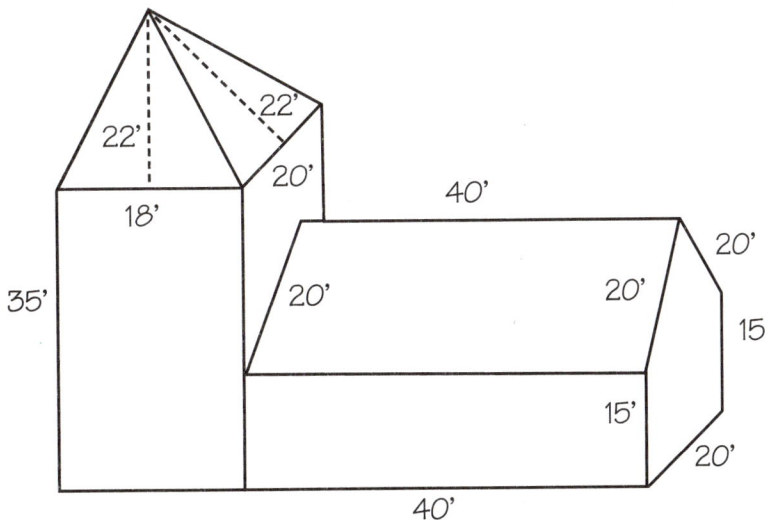

3. How many square feet of roofing will be needed for the roof of the main part of the building?

4. How many square feet of roofing will be needed for the tower roof, which is a four-sided pyramid?

5. How many square feet will the painters have to cover on the three full walls of the tower?

6. How many square feet will the painters have to cover on the two long walls of the main part of the building?

7. How many square feet will the painters have to cover on the two remaining walls? (Hint: you don't need to find the area of the triangular part of the walls.)

8. If a gallon of paint covers about 400 sq ft, about how many gallons will the painters need to cover all the outside walls of the building? (Hint: the roofs do not get painted.)

• Areas of Rectangles, Circles, and Triangles

TEST-TAKING PRACTICE

Choose the best answer for each problem. You may want to draw pictures on a separate sheet of paper. Fill in the answer box of your choice in the section at the bottom of the page.

1. What calculation would you use to find the surface area of a cube with sides measuring 10 cm?
   - A 10 x 10 + 6 = 106 sq cm
   - B 10 x 10 x 4 = 400 sq cm
   - C 10 x 10 x 6 = 600 sq cm
   - D 10 x 10 x 10 = 1,000 sq cm

2. How many square inches of paper would be used for the label on a soup can that has a radius of 2 inches and a height of 7 inches? (Use π = 22/7)
   - J 12 sq in.
   - K 24 sq in.
   - L 44 sq in.
   - M 88 sq in.

3. A box is 15 inches long, 12 inches wide, and 8 inches high. How many square inches of paper would it take to cover the box?
   - A 140 sq in.
   - B 396 sq in.
   - C 792 sq in.
   - D 1,584 sq in.

4. A book is 10 inches high and 8 inches wide. The book is 2 inches thick. How much adhesive paper would you need to cover the book?
   - J 100 sq in.
   - K 160 sq in.
   - L 180 sq in.
   - M 200 sq in.

5.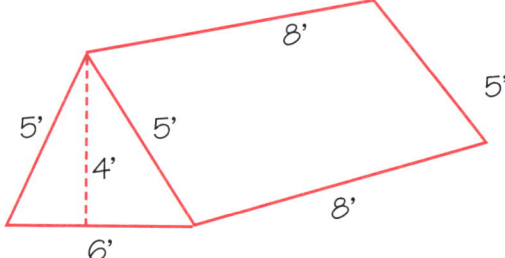

   A company is making tents like the one shown above. The tents have no floor. How much fabric will they use for each tent?
   - A 92 sq ft
   - B 104 sq ft
   - C 128 sq ft
   - D Not given

Write About It

6. A glass triangular pyramid is sitting on a table. The three faces that show are identical equilateral triangles that each have an area of 4.5 sq cm. What is the area of the hidden face? Explain your answer.

   _____

   _____

   _____

   _____

   _____

1. A☐ B☐ C☐ D☐
2. J☐ K☐ L☐ M☐
3. A☐ B☐ C☐ D☐
4. J☐ K☐ L☐ M☐
5. A☐ B☐ C☐ D☐

● Areas of Rectangles, Circles, and Triangles

Chapter 11 **L2**

Solving a Problem Within a Problem

Sometimes the information that you need to solve a problem is not given directly in the problem, in a formula, or in a diagram. To find the information, you'll have to solve another related problem first.

Example 1

The perimeter of this garden is 32 meters. What is the area of the garden?

5 m

A. **Decide what you need to find to solve the problem.**

THINK: The formula for the area of a rectangle is $A = l \times w$. I know the garden's width, so I need to find its length.

B. **Use the facts given to solve for the needed information.**

Use the formula for the perimeter of a rectangle.

$P = 2l + 2w$

$32 = 2l + (2 \times 5)$

$2l = 32 - 10 = 22$ So, $l = 11$ m

C. **Now solve the problem.**

The area of the garden $= 11 \text{ m} \times 5 \text{ m} = 55$ sq m

So, the area of the garden is 55 square meters.

Example 2

The distance around a circular pool is 44 ft. Will a square piece of canvas that has a perimeter of 48 ft cover the pool?

Step 1: You need to find the diameter of the pool. The formula for the circumference is $C = \pi d$. (Use $\pi = \frac{22}{7}$)

$C = \pi d \longrightarrow 44 = \frac{22}{7} \times d \longrightarrow d = 14$ ft

Step 2: Use the formula for the perimeter of a square to find the length of one side of the square.

$P = 4s \longrightarrow$ _____ $= 4s \longrightarrow s =$ _____

So, the canvas _____ big enough to cover the pool.

• Area, Perimeter, and Volume

GUIDED PRACTICE

1. The surface area of a cube is 54 square inches.
   What is the volume of the cube?

   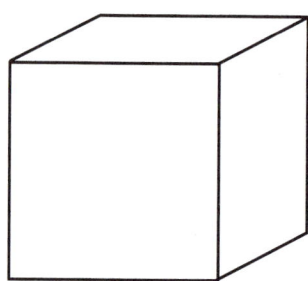

   a. Decide what you need to find to solve the problem.

      THINK: The formula for the volume of a cube is $V = s^3$.

      I need to know s, the length of each side.

   b. Use the facts given to solve for the needed information.

      Use the formula for the surface area of a cube.

      $A = 6 \times s^2$ So, _____ = $6 \times s^2$

      s^2 = _____   So, s = _____ in.

   c. Now solve the problem.

      The volume of the cube = s^3 = ___ x ___ x ___ = ___

      So, the volume of the cube is ___ cubic inches.

2. A circular ring just fits into a box that has a perimeter of 84 mm. What is the circumference of the ring? (Use $\pi = \frac{22}{7}$.)

   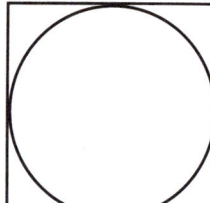

   a. Decide what you need to find to solve the problem.

      THINK: The formula for the circumference of a circle is $C = \pi d$.

      I need to know the diameter d, which equals the length of each side of the square.

   b. Use the facts given to solve for the needed information.
      Use the formula for the perimeter of a square.

      $P = 4 \times s$ → So, _____ = $4 \times s$ → So, s = _____ mm

   c. Now solve the problem.

      The circumference of the circle = πd

      Since d = s, C = _____ x _____   So, C = _____

      So, the circumference of the ring is _____ mm.

Chapter 11 | **L2**

PRACTICE

Use the formulas in the table to find the information you need to solve the problems. Show how you solved each problem.

Area	Perimeter and Circumference
Parallelogram: $A = bh$	Rectangle: $P = 2l + 2w$
Rectangle: $A = lw$	Square: $P = 4s$
Triangle: $A = \frac{1}{2}bh$	Circle: $C = 2\pi r$ or πd
Square: $A = s^2$ or $s \times s$	**Volume**
Circle: $A = \pi r^2$	Rectangular Prism: $V = lwh$
	Cube: $V = s \times s \times s$

3. The perimeter of a square building lot is 80 meters. What is the area of the lot?

4. A crate is a cube, with each side having an area of 25 sq ft. What is the volume of the crate?

5. The circumference of a circular pond is 88 meters. What is the area of the pond? (Use $\pi = 22/7$.)

6. A room that is 15 ft long has an area of 180 sq ft. What is the perimeter of the room?

7. The height of a triangular sail is twice the length of its base. If the sail is 14 ft high, what is the sail's area?

8. A box has square ends that each have an area of 121 sq in. The length of the box is 14 in. What is its volume?

● Area, Perimeter, and Volume

TEST-TAKING PRACTICE

Choose the best answer for each problem. Use the formulas if you need to. Fill in the answer box of your choice in the section at the bottom of the page.

Area
Parallelogram: .... $A = bh$
Rectangle: .... $A = lw$
Triangle: .... $A = \frac{1}{2}bh$
Square: .... $A = s^2$ or $s \times s$
Circle: .... $A = \pi r^2$

Perimeter and Circumference
Rectangle: .... $P = 2l + 2w$
Square: .... $P = 4s$
Circle .... $C = 2\pi r$ or πd

Volume
Rectangular Prism: $V = lwh$
Cube: $V = s \times s \times s$

1. The area of a circle is 154 sq cm. What would you do first if you wanted to find the circumference of the circle?
   A Solve for the volume.
   B Solve for the radius.
   C Solve for the value of π.
   D Solve for the perimeter.

2. The perimeter of the equilateral triangle is 27 cm. What is the area of the square?
   J 18 sq cm
   K 36 sq cm
   L 72 sq cm
   M 81 sq cm

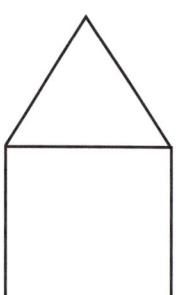

3. The distance around one face of a cube is 28 inches. What is the volume of the cube?
   A 56 cu in.   C 343 cu in.
   B 196 cu in.   D Not given

4. The area of the rectangle is 70 sq m. What is the circumference of the circle? (Use $\pi = \frac{22}{7}$.)
   J 7 m   L 14 m
   K 11 m   M 22 m

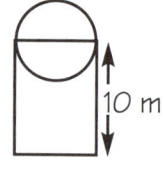

Write About It

5. One of the angles of a right triangle measures 37°. In another right triangle, one of the angles measures 53°. How could you prove that the two triangles are similar?

_____
_____
_____
_____
_____
_____

1. A☐ B☐ C☐ D☐   3. A☐ B☐ C☐ D☐
2. J☐ K☐ L☐ M☐   4. J☐ K☐ L☐ M☐

Chapter 12 | **L1**

Making an Organized List

Sometimes you must solve a math problem by finding the probability for two independent events. You can start by making an organized list of all possible outcomes. Then you can use the list to solve the problem.

Example 1

Suppose you draw a letter from Box 1 and a letter from Box 2. How many possible outcomes are there?

Box 1	Box 2
A R T	S C I E N C E

To find **all** the possible outcomes, make an organized list.

Step 1: Match the *A* from Box 1 with each letter from Box 2:
(A,S) (A,C) (A, I) (A,E) (A,N) (A,C) (A, E)

Step 2: Match the *R* from Box 1 with each letter from Box 2:
(R,S) (R,C) (R, I) (R,E) (R,N) (R,C) (R, E)

Step 3: Match the *T* from Box 1 with each letter from Box 2:

_____

Step 4: Count all the possible outcomes.

There are _____ possible outcomes.

Example 2

Suppose you draw a letter from Box 1 and a letter from Box 2. What is the probability that you will draw two vowels?

Step 1: Look at the organized list you made for Example 1. Find all the outcomes with two vowels. Write them on the lines.

_____ _____ _____

Step 2: Count the outcomes with two vowels.

There are _____ outcomes with two vowels.

Step 3: Solve. Find the probability of drawing two vowels.

Probability of drawing two vowels = $\dfrac{\text{Number of outcomes with two vowels}}{\text{Number of all possible outcomes}}$

So, the probability of drawing two vowels is $\dfrac{}{21}$, or $\dfrac{}{7}$.

• Simple Probability

GUIDED PRACTICE

What are the possible outcomes if you spin each of the two spinners at the right? Make an organized list to find all of the possible outcomes.

Spinner A

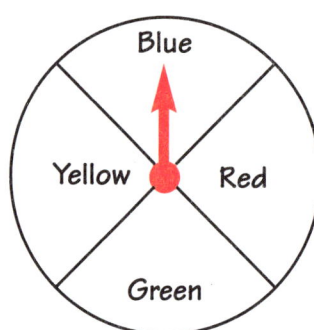

1. Match Blue on Spinner A with each color on Spinner B.

   _____

2. Match Red on Spinner A with each color on Spinner B.

   _____

Spinner B

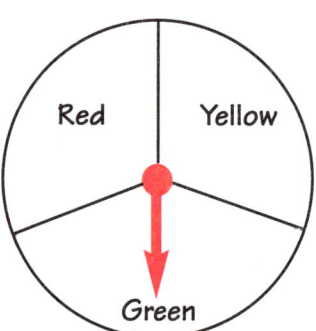

3. Match Green on Spinner A with each color on Spinner B.

   _____

4. Match Yellow on Spinner A with each color on Spinner B.

   _____

Use your list of possible outcomes to answer the questions below.

5. How many possible outcomes are there for the two spinners?

   _____

6. What is the probability that at least one of the colors spun will be yellow?

   _____

7. What is the probability of spinning a blue and a red?

   _____

8. What is the probability of getting a blue on Spinner A and any other color on Spinner B?

   _____

9. What is the probability of spinning the same color on both spinners?

   _____

10. What is the probability of getting a red on one spinner and a green on the other?

    _____

Chapter 12 | **L1**

PRACTICE

Make an organized list to solve the problems.

For problems 11–13, suppose you toss the number cube and flip the coin. The number cube is numbered from 1 to 6.

11. List all the possible outcomes.

_____

_____

12. What is the probability of tossing an even number and a head?

_____

13. What is the probability of getting a 2 and a tail?

_____

For problems 14–20, suppose that you draw a marble out of each jar.

14. List all the possible outcomes.

_____

_____

_____

_____

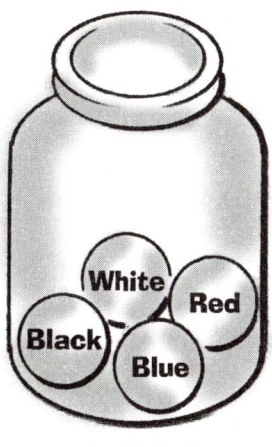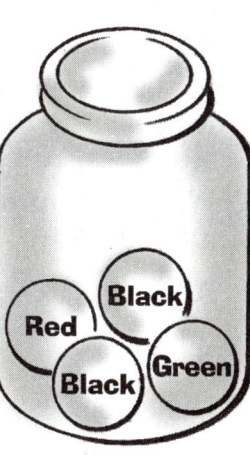

15. What is the probability of drawing a white marble and a green marble?

_____

16. What is the probability of drawing two black marbles?

_____

17. What is the probability of drawing at least one red marble?

_____

18. What is the probability of drawing exactly one black marble?

_____

19. What is the probability of drawing two marbles the same color?

_____

20. What is the probability of drawing two red marbles?

_____

• Simple Probability

TEST-TAKING PRACTICE

Choose the best answer for each problem. In the answer section at the bottom of the page, fill in the box of your choice.

For Problems 1–5, suppose you spin each of the spinners shown.

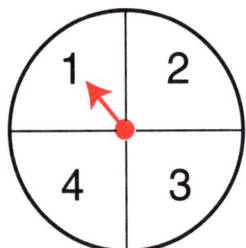
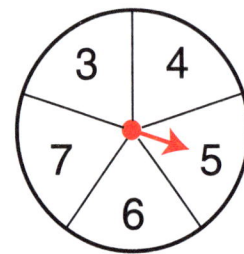

1. How many outcomes are possible?
   A 7
   B 9
   C 16
   D 20

2. For how many outcomes are both of the numbers the same?
   J 1
   K 2
   L 4
   M 5

3. What is the probability of spinning a 1 and a 5?
   A $\frac{1}{20}$
   B $\frac{1}{10}$
   C $\frac{1}{5}$
   D $\frac{1}{4}$

4. What is the probability of spinning two even numbers?
   J $\frac{1}{20}$
   K $\frac{1}{10}$
   L $\frac{1}{5}$
   M $\frac{1}{4}$

5. What is the probability of spinning a 3 and a 4?
   A $\frac{1}{20}$
   B $\frac{1}{10}$
   C $\frac{1}{5}$
   D Not given

Write About It

6. Suppose you toss two number cubes. Each cube has six sides numbered from 1 to 6. How would you make an organized list to show all the possible outcomes?

_____
_____
_____
_____
_____
_____
_____
_____
_____
_____
_____

---

1. A ☐ B ☐ C ☐ D ☐
2. J ☐ K ☐ L ☐ M ☐
3. A ☐ B ☐ C ☐ D ☐
4. J ☐ K ☐ L ☐ M ☐
5. A ☐ B ☐ C ☐ D ☐

• Simple Probability

Chapter 12 | **L2**

Making a Tree Diagram

If you need to find all the outcomes for three or more independent events, making an organized list may be difficult. To show all of the possible outcomes in an organized way, make a tree diagram.

Example

If you spin the three spinners shown at right, what is the probability that at least two of the spinners will point to red?

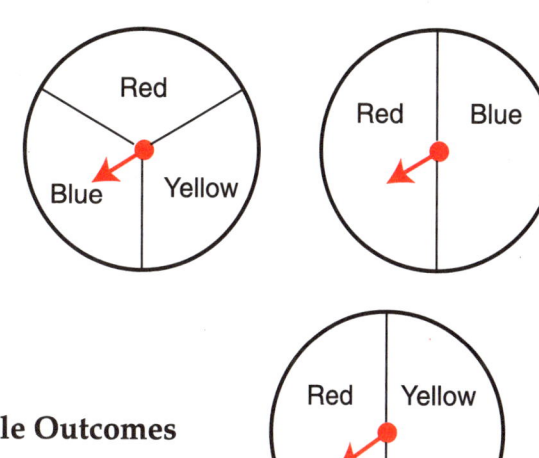

A. Complete the tree diagram to show all possible outcomes.

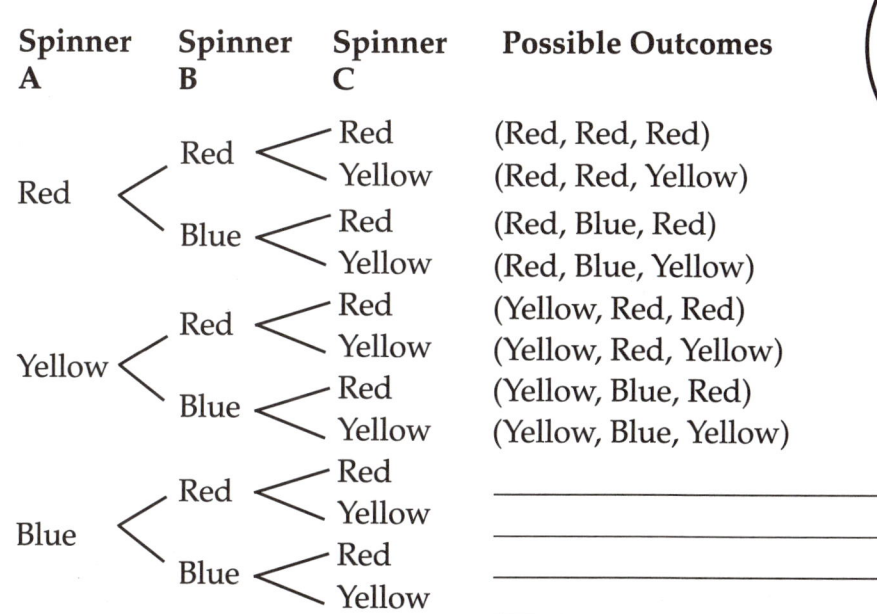

Spinner A	Spinner B	Spinner C	Possible Outcomes
Red	Red	Red	(Red, Red, Red)
		Yellow	(Red, Red, Yellow)
	Blue	Red	(Red, Blue, Red)
		Yellow	(Red, Blue, Yellow)
Yellow	Red	Red	(Yellow, Red, Red)
		Yellow	(Yellow, Red, Yellow)
	Blue	Red	(Yellow, Blue, Red)
		Yellow	(Yellow, Blue, Yellow)
Blue	Red	Red	_____
		Yellow	_____
	Blue	Red	_____
		Yellow	_____

B. Count the possible outcomes for all three spinners.

How many possible outcomes are there? _____

C. Find the possible outcomes with at least two spinners pointing to red.

How many are there? _____

D. Solve the problem.

What is the probability that at least two of the spinners will point to red?

_____

• Simple Probability

GUIDED PRACTICE

Use a tree diagram to solve the problems.

1. If you toss four coins, what is the probability that exactly three of them will land heads up?

   Step 1: Complete the tree diagram to show all possible outcomes.

Coin 1	Coin 2	Coin 3	Coin 4	Possible Outcomes

   HHHH
   _____
   _____
   _____
   _____
   _____
   _____
   _____
   _____
   _____
   _____
   _____
   _____
   _____
   _____
   _____

   Step 2: Count all the possible outcomes for tossing the four coins. What is the total number of possible outcomes?

   _____

   Step 3: Count the outcomes with exactly three heads. How many are there?

   _____

   Step 4: Solve. If you toss four coins, what is the probability that exactly three of them will land heads up?

   _____

2. If you toss four coins, what is the probability that at least two of them will land heads up? Hint: Count all the possibilities with two or more heads.

   _____

Chapter 12 L2

PRACTICE

Suppose you draw one letter from each bag.

3. **Make a tree diagram to show all of the possible outcomes.**

Bag 1   Bag 2   Bag 3   Possible Outcomes

Use the tree diagram to find each probability if you draw one letter from each bag.

4. **What is the probability of drawing at least one *O*?**

   _____

5. **What is the probability of drawing an *N* and an *O* (in any order)?**

   _____

6. **What is the probability of drawing at least two consonants?**

   _____

7. **What is the probability that all three letters drawn will be different letters?**

   _____

8. **What is the probability of drawing exactly two *O*'s?**

   _____

9. **What is the probability of NOT drawing a *G*?**

   _____

• Simple Probability

173

TEST-TAKING PRACTICE

Choose the best answer for each problem. In the answer section at the bottom of the page, fill in the box of your choice.

For Problems 1–5, suppose you draw one straw from each glass without looking.

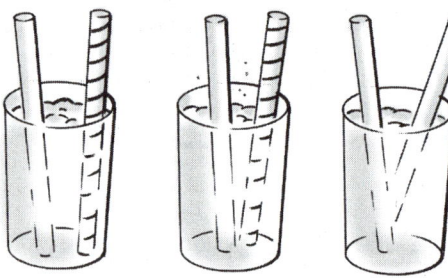

1. How many possible outcomes are there?
   A 4
   B 8
   C 12
   D 16

2. For how many outcomes is exactly one straw striped?
   J 2
   K 6
   L 4
   M 8

3. What is the probability that exactly two of the three straws drawn will be plain?
   A $\frac{1}{8}$
   B $\frac{1}{4}$
   C $\frac{3}{8}$
   D $\frac{1}{2}$

4. What is the probability that all three straws will be the same?
   J $\frac{1}{8}$
   K $\frac{1}{4}$
   L $\frac{1}{2}$
   M $\frac{5}{8}$

5. What is the probability that at least one straw is plain?
   A $\frac{1}{4}$
   B $\frac{1}{2}$
   C $\frac{3}{4}$
   D Not given

Write About It
Write a plan for solving the following problem. Then solve.

6. Suppose you draw one card from three boxes. The first box contains the letters *A* and *T*. The second box contains the letters *T* and *O*. The third box contains the letters *A* and *N*. What is the probability that you will draw at least one vowel?

_____

_____

_____

_____

_____

_____

_____

_____

_____

_____

1. A☐ B☐ C☐ D☐
2. J☐ K☐ L☐ M☐
3. A☐ B☐ C☐ D☐
4. J☐ K☐ L☐ M☐
5. A☐ B☐ C☐ D☐

• Simple Probability

Chapters 1–12

Test-Taking Skill: Trying Out the Answer Choices

If you have trouble solving a multiple choice problem, try out the answer choices. It can help you find the correct answer.

Example 1

A circle has a circumference of 44 centimeters. Which of the following is the most reasonable estimate of the circle's diameter?

    A 7 cm   **C** 14 cm

    B 10 cm   **D** 21 cm

Step 1: Try out each answer in the equation $C = \pi d$.

Use 3 as an approximate value of π.

Answer A: $3 \times 7 = 21$ cm   **This is too small for a reasonable estimate.**

Answer B: $3 \times 10 = 30$ cm   **This estimate seems a bit low.**

Answer C: $3 \times 14 = 42$ cm   **This estimate is very close.**

Answer D: $3 \times 21 = 63$ cm   **This is too large for a reasonable estimate.**

Step 2: Choose the estimate that's closest to the actual circumference.

The correct answer is _____.

Example 2

A 30-minute television show has 20 commercials. On average, how many commercials is that per minute of the show?

    A $\frac{1}{2}$ **C** 2.3

    B $\frac{2}{3}$ **D** 20

Step 1: Try out each answer choice as a proportion of commercials/min.

Answer A: $\frac{1}{2}$ = 15 commercials/30 min

This is not the correct proportion.

Answer B: $\frac{2}{3}$ = 20 commercials/30 min

This is the correct proportion: 20 commercial per 30 minutes.

Step 2: You've found the correct answer, so you don't need to keep trying.

The correct answer is _____.

• Test-Taking Skill

TEST-TAKING PRACTICE

Choose the best answer for each problem. In the answer section at the bottom of the page, fill in the box of your choice.

1. Brian can read about 35 pages per hour. How many hours would it take for him to finish a 210-page book?

   A 6 hours   C 10 hours
   B 7 hours   D 35 pages

2. The area of a rectangle is 918 square inches. Its length is 34 inches. What is the width of the rectangle?

   J 2.7 in.   L 884 sq in.
   K 27 in.   M Not given

3. A couch that was marked $418 was discounted $65. By about what percent was the price reduced?

   A 5%   C 15%
   B 10%   D 20%

4. The volume of a cube is 421.875 cubic centimeters. What is the length of each side of the cube?

   J 2.5 cm   L 7.5 cm
   K 6.5 cm   M 20.5 cm

5. Julio bought 3 cassettes at the regular price, and one cassette that was $2 less than the regular price. He paid a total of $31.00. What was the regular price of a cassette?

   A $6.25   C $8.00
   B $7.75   D $8.25

6. Bo thought of a number. He doubled it, then added 10. Then he divided the sum by 4, and ended up with 6. What number did Bo think of?

   J 6   L 9
   K 7   M 15

7. You are a contestant in the "Guess Again—It's Math" show. The announcer gives the radius of a circle as 2.8 inches, and asks what the amount 24.64 would represent in the circle. What should you answer?

   A the diameter, in inches
   B the circumference, in inches
   C the area, in square inches
   D Not given

1. A☐ B☐ C☐ D☐   5. A☐ B☐ C☐ D☐
2. J☐ K☐ L☐ M☐   6. J☐ K☐ L☐ M☐
3. A☐ B☐ C☐ D☐   7. A☐ B☐ C☐ D☐
4. J☐ K☐ L☐ M☐

● Test-Taking Skill